A Different Joy

Acclaim for *A Different Joy: The Parents' Guide to Living Better with Autism, ADHD, Dyslexia and more...*

"As a small package can contain a very valuable present, this is a small book that contains valuable information for parents. The descriptions, explanations and strategies are clear and perceptive such that this is the 'go to' book for parents and grandparents. I especially appreciated the positive attitude and emphasis on the abilities and qualities of children who have autism." – Tony Attwood, Author of *The Complete Guide to Asperger Syndrome*.

"Warm-hearted book for parents of newly diagnosed autistic children with plenty of sensible advice." – Shannon Coles

"Easy read and a must read for anyone trying to understand this confusing world." – Fiona Barclay, parent

"It is a very, very good read, with a warm, informal, personal tone and a solid professional base. I just wish I had read this when I was Home Start volunteer to a distressed mother with two demanding under 5s. I'll send a link to her straight away!" – Former Home Start Volunteer

"In this wonderfully positive and insightful book, Sarah-Jane Critchley looks in depth at issues that parents of children with special educational needs (SEN) face. Unlike other books which can be overly academic and impenetrable, this book is full of real life examples and practical advice. As a parent of children with SEN herself, Sarah-Jane is a very credible guide through the complicated world of special needs. She isn't just a professional in the field, she has lived it. Here she shares lessons learned and strategies that have helped in a way that encourages and supports but never preaches or patronises. What is comforting about this book as it takes the emphasis off of trying to be a 'perfect parent'. Bringing up a child with special needs is often trial and error, and Sarah-Jane is refreshingly honest about strategies and approaches that have worked for her as well as outlining times when things haven't worked out. I know a lot of parents will take great comfort from this." – Dean Beadle, International lecturer in Asperger syndrome.

"This book is nurturing like a good cup of tea.

"Reading this book through the eyes of a professional in the field of autism, I was struck by its openness, honesty and very human approach. It takes you on a journey of living with and supporting children who see and experience the world differently from pre diagnosis until adulthood. At each stage of the journey Sarah has shared personal and professional experiences, a wealth of practical tips, resources and sign posting in such an accessible way. This is an excellent book for parents to support them on their own journey but also for professionals to gain a clear and honest insight into the lives of children with additional needs and their families.

"This book champions difference, that nobody is perfect and celebrates children for who they are. I will be recommending this book to the families and settings my team support." – Clare Henshaw, Autism Outreach Coordinator, Brent Outreach Autism Team.

"If ever there was a truer sentence than this, I can't think of it, 'People are never a simple proposition, we are a complex, messy combination of the genes we were given, what happened to us in our lives from conception onwards and our experiences – all of which combine to make us the people we are.'

"Life is messy. Art is messy. Science is messy, and the surest way to make God laugh is to tell him our plans – because heavens are THEY messy!

"Sarah-Jane Critchley's *A Different Joy* asks 'whoever said there were boxes into which we SHOULD fit anyway?' Offering both practical and personal resilience for turning messy into 'mess-tastic'." – Jennifer Cook O'Toole, Temple Grandin Outstanding Literary Work of the Year and Bestselling *Asperkids* series, Aspie, Mom.

About the Author

Sarah-Jane is the mother of two delightful and unusual children. Her childhood was largely free range and spanned schooling in Birmingham and holidays on the family farm in Shropshire. She was the SEN Governor for an infant school and a volunteer in the local branch of the National Association for Gifted Children (NAGC). For the last seven years she has worked within the autism sector and as a representative of her organisation has been consulted in connection with reviews of SEN policy and implementation for the UK government. She is a part of international collaborations working to share her organisation's autism training programme with Italy, Greece and China.

She loves to balance her passion for work with her family and she enjoys a broad range of hobbies including sailing, singing, writing poetry and learning new things. She stands five foot seven inches tall (on tip toes) with brown hair, hazel eyes and shares her first name with Doctor Who companion, Sarah-Jane Smith.

Within her extended family she has a fascinating combination of conditions including autism, dyslexia, ADHD (inattentiveness rather than hyperactivity), dyspraxia, schizophrenia and depression which has given her a personal perspective on the challenges that families face.

A Different Joy

The Parents' Guide to Living Better with
Autism, ADHD, Dyslexia and more…

Sarah-Jane Critchley

Illustrations by E.M. Critchley

To my darling David, Beth & Alex. You bring me so much joy daily. I love you, come what may.

To my extended family and my closest friends, those who are here and those who have gone on before, you have given me so much time, space, love and a refuge when I needed it. Thank you.

Contents

Chapter 3: Know Your Child

Chapter 8: Perfect Schools Don't Exist. How to Find the the Best You Can

Chapter 9: Bullying, Vulnerability and Resilience

Chapter 10: From Surviving To Thriving

Glossary of Terms and Titles   170

Foreword by Dean Beadle

Parenting a child with special needs is a complex task. I should know, I was a special needs child who was complex to parent! With a diagnosis of Asperger syndrome, my parents faced many challenges in bringing me up. My socially inappropriate behaviours led to me being frequently suspended from school and my obsessive interest in Doctor Who made me not only difficult but expensive!

I know that when my mum first got my diagnosis she had several unanswered questions. What would the future be like for her child? Would I have the same opportunities as other people? Thankfully, if you are reading this as a parent of a newly diagnosed child, you are on the right track to putting these fears to bed.

In this wonderfully positive and insightful book, Sarah-Jane Critchley looks in depth at issues that parents of children with special educational needs (SEN) face. Unlike other books which can be overly academic and impenetrable, this book is full of real life examples and practical advice. As a parent of children with SEN herself, Sarah-Jane is a very credible guide through the complicated world of special needs. She isn't just a professional in the field, she has lived it. Here she shares lessons learned and strategies that have helped in a way that encourages and supports but never preaches or patronises. What is comforting about this book as it takes the emphasis off of trying to be 'a perfect parent'. Bringing up a child with special needs is often trial and error, and Sarah-Jane is refreshingly honest about strategies and approaches that have worked for her as well as outlining times when things haven't worked out. I know a lot of parents will take great comfort from this.

This book would be an excellent starting point for any parent entering the world of SEN. By the time you get to the last page, I'm sure you will feel informed, inspired and well-equipped to continue to meet your unique young person's needs. Because after all, parenting a child with special needs may be complex but it's also incredibly rewarding (of course I'm biased!).

Dean Beadle

International lecturer in Asperger syndrome

Acknowledgements

I would like to thank the many friends who have shared details of their lives, their concerns, their fears and their triumphs. I am so thankful for my colleagues in the world of autism and special educational needs who have been an inspiration over the last seven years. They have given me a master class in theory, practice, generosity, and made a difference in the lives of some of our most vulnerable people. I have been privileged to meet doctors, practitioners, teachers and other professionals that I have met as a parent, professional or SEN school governor. They have taught me so much about my own and other people's children. I am delighted and cheered by the commitment, resourcefulness and passion of many of the people who work with our children. A heartfelt thank you to you all.

Thanks to the lovely people who helped me choose the title of the book from the cornucopia of options whizzing round my head, and all the people who have encouraged me along the way, especially those who gave me permission to include them by name in the book. Special thanks go to my wonderful panel of readers, Fiona Barklay, David Critchley, Joanne Driver, Steve Jones, Jane Mars and the wonderful Dean Beadle who has also been kind enough to contribute the foreword. I am especially delighted with the wonderful illustrations drawn by my daughter specifically for this book. My darling Beth, you are a star! Please note that any errors in spelling, grammar or punctuation are all mine, and are there specifically to make those of you who enjoy looking for them happy. They are nothing to do with Annette Grey who contributed her excellent proof-reading skills!

My greatest love, adoration and thanks go to my family and my husband who have been hugely supportive, but most especially my children who are doing a great job of bringing me up as a parent. We learn together. I am lost in admiration for the people they are turning into.

How to use this book

I have written this book primarily for parents at the beginning of their understanding of special needs. For those of you who know a little, or a lot more, there is always something new to learn and something new to try. I would suggest starting with Chapter 1 which gives you an overview of the book, but I understand that some of you will be too busy and stressed out to do that! Feel free to drop into any area that you feel will help you using the contents page. Each chapter has footnotes throughout the text with links and references that you can follow to find further information and support. There is a lot of specialist terminology in the world of special needs, so I have included a glossary of terms at the back of the book. This book was designed to give you the most up to date support and all links worked at the time of publication. If for any reason a link has stopped working (as they will as websites change) just use your search engine to find it (or something like it). Most importantly, make yourself a cup of something cheering, sit down, relax and enjoy.

Chapter 1

An Introduction to Sane-ish Parenting

Who am I and why did I write this book?

I am a parent of children with special needs who has worked in the autism sector for the last seven years putting training, tools and resources into the hands of teachers and people working with teachers in schools. My experience as a professional has been dramatically different to my reality as a parent. As a professional I am well-trained, well supported, and have a host of resources at my disposal. As a parent I have often felt isolated, de-skilled and disempowered. There is much less support available for parents. I have had my dark days when I really felt that I couldn't cope and was hanging on by my fingernails. I know that you will fight for your children if you must, but how desperately you want it to be unnecessary. I have met people through my work who have inspired me and would like to share their stories with you. When I look at my children, I see people with huge potential whose unique strengths lie within their differences. We need to work to create a world where that view is shared by the majority of society.

I am far from being a perfect parent as I am sure my children would tell you! I write this book not as an expert, but as someone who travels through life just doing the best they can. I hope that what I have learned might help you. We all make mistakes and I confess to being fully human. In doing so it is entirely possible that I might upset some of you, and that you might not agree with what I say. If I do, I am sorry if it causes you any distress, please accept that this is not intentional. We are all different and what works for one of us, may not work for someone else. I'm always willing to listen, and learn, so please share any good ideas that you have. What tools, skills and resources I have, grew out of problems I resolved thanks to the kindness and generosity of others sharing their experience and knowledge. I'm hugely grateful for the help I've received. Please use what you read and hear to help you and don't forget to share the good as well as the bad with the people around you. Spread a little joy wherever you go whenever you can.

My one wish for you is that you use what I have written to make your lives, and those of your children easier, happier, and more fulfilling.

What all parents want for their children – happiness

In many ways, it feels as if the job of a parent is simply learning how to fail in new and different ways to your parents. It is the original definition of an impossible job. One that is 24 hours a day, seven days a week for the rest of your life. You get the incredibly precious gift of a small defenceless person and the opportunity to help them grow into an adult. The 'easy' bit is when your children are in the womb, and all you have to do is eat the right things, drink the right things and do the right things! Even at that stage, a significant proportion of the person that they will become was hardwired into their DNA. Once they are born and developing into children, you have the false impression that you can control the people that they will be. As a keen observer of my own and other people's children, I'm very aware that each child is their own person first and foremost. All that we can do is support the way that they develop. Even as we accept that we aren't the only influence, we need to realise just how important the role of a parent is on a young person, even if our role decreases as our children get older.

The vast majority of parents would say that happiness for their children is more important than academic achievement, financial or social goals. Growing up is a scary proposition for a child. They have little control over their lives. They are meeting new challenges in terms of understanding other people, school, and the world around them on a daily basis. New ideas challenge what they know, and exciting opportunities present themselves, but they also learn that things go wrong and that they will fail. When this happens children need a stable, safe place to return to – somewhere where they know they are loved and cherished. That is why small children often have a favourite toy that they have to carry everywhere. Their constant companion makes the rapidly changing world a much less frightening place. There is reassurance in the predictability of repetition, whether it's a favourite TV programme, or much loved book which they ask for again and again.

The problem is that try as you might, loving as you are, life just doesn't go smoothly all the time. Unless you're that incredibly fortunate person who leads a charmed life, you will have things that go wrong, challenge you and undermine your ability to be the parent you want to be. Troubles come into our lives unasked for and unwanted, but we have to deal with them as best we can. Some of us become ill, lose loved ones, our jobs or our homes. Stress impacts our family as a whole. I find it is better to accept that you can fail to be perfect, but succeed in showing your young people that things go wrong, they can survive them, and through it all they are loved. There is huge power in being a good enough parent and modelling how to be imperfect!

Love is a long-term proposition – doing the long haul without burning out

Life can be very hard sometimes. The children have their own problems and put you under almost intolerable pressure either intentionally or through no fault of their own from time to time. In the hurly-burly whirl of day-to-day life, it is easy to spend all your time sorting out everybody else and forget about your own needs. You wouldn't expect your car to run without petrol, so why would you expect yourself to run continually without putting anything back into your physical, emotional, and spiritual tanks?

As in any long-term battle or campaign it is helpful to have a plan. It can sometimes feel as if you are buried in worries about what's gone wrong, and what on earth is going to happen in the future. To do that effectively, you need to build a picture that you can communicate with other people who are working with your child, around what they like, what they know, what their strengths are and what they need help with. A pupil profile such as the examples in the Autism Education Trust's Standards, Matthew's passport[1] and Joe's passport[2] are helpful in describing your child to other people. Once you know their strengths it becomes easier to build on those for the future. Starting from where you want your child to be is a great way to think about what they need in order to help them get there. You can break any plan into short, medium and long-term goals. The art is in combining those goals into where you want to get to. Once you've identified what it is that you and your child want, it becomes far easier to get there!

---

1 www.aettraininghubs.org.uk/wp-content/uploads/2012/05/1.1-matthews_passport.pdf

2 www.aettraininghubs.org.uk/wp-content/uploads/2012/05/1.2-joes_passport.pdf

We all need a little help along the way. There is a saying that it takes a village to raise a child. Although few of us live in village communities any more, we are all part of large and small groups whether these are schools, clubs, churches or the places where we live. The people we have contact with can bring joy to our days and provide us with perspectives that can be hugely helpful. Any parent who discovers their child has special needs is likely to have access to a range of healthcare professionals who can help to identify what the issues are and signpost towards additional support.

Divorce, separation and mental health

It is a sad fact of life that many families find that they cannot live together any more. When the additional pressures of raising a child with special educational needs or disability are added on top of the pressures of everyday life, divorce and separation are understandable. They are even more likely, but are not inevitable. The strains of dealing with a young person with special needs tend not to fall equally on both partners within a relationship. It is usually, but not always, the mother of the child who spends more time with them and is more likely to recognise the difference between their child and others of a similar age. This is because mothers tend to be better connected in terms of pre-and postnatal care and playgroups to other mothers – whereas more fathers take the role of lead provider and tend to be less involved in childcare. Men seek help less often and therefore receive less support. The combination of these factors make it less likely that fathers will recognise difference in terms of what their child is doing in comparison to other children, and more likely that they will struggle with a diagnosis.

We often hear from mothers who say that their partner won't accept that there is an issue because they were like that when they were little, so that is normal isn't it? If the mother pursues diagnosis it can be perceived by the father as an overt criticism of him, his genetic makeup and his family, although this is almost never what's intended. Both men and women hate to hear of anything being wrong with their children, but men struggle particularly when it isn't something they don't know how to fix. For both parents, there is the fear of what a diagnosis might mean for the future of their child. If parents don't agree on the best thing to do, it is completely normal for there to be conflict which puts the relationship under strain. Whilst support for parents is patchy and depends on where you live, there is less help specifically for fathers. You wouldn't see most men flocking to all women groups, so why would it be any different just because they have a child with special needs?

Most assistance available to parents is not specific to the type of special need, and there are particular worries, that only a parent of a child in a similar position will understand. It is also true that many children with special needs have behaviours that challenge adults and children around them, which all too often leads to them being isolated or excluded from the normal social groups. This is when it's good to find other people in similar positions.

Parenting special needs children is hard! – taking care of yourself

When you try and work out what's going on with your child and how to make their life easier, it is all about them. All your energies go into trying to work out what it is, how to deal with it, and what is the best thing to do next. There is often little space for anything else. There have been days, weeks and months and years when I have felt like life is one long laundry list of things that have to be done – when stuff I wanted didn't even get on the list. As children get older though, it does get easier for most people. Although far from perfect and sometimes far from good, I have noticed that when I take time for myself I'm better at doing things for my children.

One of the greatest gifts I have been given, is to understand the calming and helpful role of routines in running a household with autism in the family. Planning and preparation moves us through the days far more happily with less stress. It isn't that we couldn't manage before, but I noticed that I'm much calmer, less grumpy and shout less when things are sorted in advance. Even so, I don't manage to do it all the time, however much I know that it helps! Learning better ways of organising myself, my children and the house has been a huge blessing to me. As someone with ADD tendencies myself, I love the 'Do It Now' principle[3] which helps me to do things before I get distracted

3 The 'Do It Now' principle says that if something needs to be done, you should do it

by the next thing! When planning, don't forget to build in time for yourself on the calendar so that it happens.

One in four people will suffer from mental health illness in their lifetime. That figure is much higher for parents of children with special needs and for mothers reporting clinical levels of depression the figure is over 50%.[4] Our health also impacts on that of our children, so it is doubly important that we take care of ourselves, especially when they are dependent on us to take care of them. Recognising that reality, and learning to deal with it is an important part of getting the help you need.

It's a family affair – siblings, parents, and other animals

Many neurodevelopmental conditions including autism seem to run in families and there is a genetic component to the condition, although that is by no means the single cause. If you're ever a visitor in another family, you notice how different families are to each other. The rules change, behaviours change, what is tolerated and what is encouraged can vary dramatically from family to family. At its best, the family can provide a safe, secure environment where difference is understood and valued, and where responsibilities for raising a child can be shared and everyone works as a team. Unfortunately, this isn't always the case and many single parents are left to manage a very demanding child and their siblings. Having a brother or sister who is different can also be very difficult. Unless handled carefully, it can rob them of having a clean start to become the person they want to be if they follow an older brother or sister to the same school. In some cases siblings are carers too. Many siblings speak positively and with great love about the experience of having a brother or sister with a disability.

There are two main psychological drives in terms of identity; the drive to belong and the drive to be an individual. When family bonds are really strong it gives young people a solid base from which to become

---

straight away before you forget. If it can't be done straight away, use a diary, calendar, or post-it note to remind yourself not to forget.

4 Bromley, Jo et al. (2004) Mothers Supporting Children with Autism: Social Support, mental health status and satisfaction with services in *Autism*. Sage and the National Autistic Society. Vol 8 (4) 409-423.

the individuals they are destined to become. The family is the first place where we learn to work with other people. It delivers a long-term interpersonal training programme that will affect our communication style for good or ill. A lot of communication and social skills training can happen over the dining table. Studies have shown that the eldest[5] child learns how to talk from parents, and younger children learn more complex language from their older siblings than from adults.

The family also offers lots of opportunity to reward good behaviour. If you have a plan in place that suggests that you will get the children to do more chores around the house, and you spot one of them doing something good, then you are in position to be able to reward them. As the saying goes, 'You catch more flies with honey than with vinegar'. Although it doesn't work all the time, it is slightly better than continual nagging.

To diagnose or not to diagnose? That is the question!

Having discovered that something isn't right, whether it's because someone has noticed that there's something different about your child or whether it's your gut instinct, you then have to decide what you do with that information and whether you're going to explore more. One of the most important decisions you have to make is whether to seek diagnosis or not. My own experience has been rather mixed. It took us a couple of years, multiple visits to healthcare professionals, a lot of soul-searching and a huge amount of emotional turmoil to get to the point of diagnosis the first time round. We were given a diagnosis, offered medication to drug our child into learning 'normally' and referred to a book detailing all of the ways that our adored child's brain was 'not working'. As parents, we were given no help, no hope and nothing positive about the different strengths that come with being wired differently. So we did not seek any sort of diagnosis for our second child despite quite obvious differences until they were close to leaving primary school.

What we do know is that an early diagnosis and appropriate help leads to better outcomes for children (although it is never too late to

---

5 *The Effect of Birth Order on Emerging Language* by Lauren Lowry, Hanen SLP and clinical writer www.hanen.org/SiteAssets/Helpful-Info/Articles/the-effect-of-birth-order.aspx

make a difference). Having a diagnosis can be a gateway to additional services designed specifically for children with those particular issues, but only if they are available locally. In a world of limited resources, diagnosis is often the way that local authorities decide whether support is available or not. Even when this isn't the case, knowing the nature of your child's condition will help you to find solutions that work far more effectively. In all of the areas of Special Educational Need and Disability (SEND), there are many different things that you can do, but you have to know what condition(s) you are dealing with first. There is a wealth of resources and information available on the Internet, at least some of which is both reliable and helpful. What is available varies from condition to condition.

All children need to be able to communicate effectively, whether that is verbally, in writing or using a different way to communicate. They might find this hard if they have a speech, language and communication need (SLCN).[6] A child who can't communicate finds it hard to learn and the child's ability to progress at the same speed as their peers is affected. Adults with autism and dyslexia have said time and again how they felt stupid and were called slow. It had a negative impact on their ability to learn, their lives at school, and whether they were bullied. Diagnosis is a gateway to understanding and acceptance of not only the issues around condition, but also the strengths that their differences can bring.

Learning about your children so you can advocate for them

Most parents can leave it up to their children to find their own way through life, but if you are a parent of a child who has special needs then you already know that you are not most parents! I've noticed a watchful attentiveness in some parents of children with autism where they observe the child's behaviour and what it says about what is going on. Parents use that information to understand and interpret for a child who is not always able to express for themselves what is

---

6 Speech, Language and Communication needs general but recognised term for a range of communication issues. A child with speech, language and communication needs might have speech that is difficult to understand, might struggle to say words or sentences, may not understand words that are being used, or the instructions they hear, or may have difficulties knowing how to talk and listen to others in a conversation.

happening. There are lots of different ways of parenting children and each parent has to choose their own style to match their own needs and those of their children. The one that doesn't work with children with autism and organisational skills issues is just leaving them to get on with it. Without your help, care and intervention they will really struggle to make sense of the world and their place in it. Whilst the vast majority of young people can learn to function very well, they will need to be taught explicitly in detail about the way that people work. Children with dyslexia need to have language and writing in particular decoded for them so they can understand how to use words effectively.

It makes it very hard for you to be able to support your children effectively if you don't understand what they are experiencing when they interact with the world. I have been struck repeatedly by how sophisticated and effective the alternative communication methods used by some professionals can be and how rarely parents are given the same training opportunities. A good communication mechanism can make a massive difference in young person's life. It can be the gateway to their independence and their ability to express their thoughts, wishes and desires.

As a parent we are ideally placed to really watch and learn everything about our children, the unique set of conditions and the specific combinations of strengths and weaknesses that they have and the delightful people that they are. Very often children with one area of special need will have other issues to keep it company, and it is often a combination between two or more conditions that shapes the profile of difficulties and strengths that young person has. The more you know the more you can help. There is a lot of information available on all medical conditions on the Internet these days, and although it can be hard to find a local group providing support for a particular condition, there are many support groups online for parents and for individuals themselves.

Communicating with children who find talking difficult

With some children all we need to do is ask. But for others, who may not feel ready to talk about these things, or may not be able to talk, then it takes more effort. Even if your child can speak, it is really easy to get into a position where all the conversations that you have with your child are about what they need to do, school, or why they haven't tidied their room! It is far harder to have conversations with them about their hopes, dreams, relationships and sex, or where they are struggling when they want to be independent. If you never have those sort of conversations with them it is really hard, because sometimes parents we don't know how to start those conversations either. We are usually more skilled at difficult conversations than our children are and they need our help to be able to do that.

But what if they can't tell you in words? What if they don't speak are clearly or aren't able to express themselves? Then there are plenty of other techniques you can use to communicate with them and find out from them what they enjoy and what they want. Augmentative and alternative communication (AAC)[7] is a term used to describe a wide range of communication methods used by people who find it difficult to produce or understand spoken or written language. Some of the methods most often used include:

1. **Sign languages such as Makaton**[8] – Makaton is a language program using signs and symbols to help people to communicate. It is designed to help support spoken language and the signs and symbols are used in spoken word order. Some parents have found it very helpful when a child is late in developing spoken language, to reduce frustration and help their communication. It is also in use in some schools to support children with special needs, especially in inclusive classrooms.

2. **Talking mats**[9] – Talking mats are a communication symbols tool designed by speech and language therapists that can be used to help children and young people express their thoughts, preferences and feelings both positive and negative. It is been used to consult children and young people especially in terms of their individual education plan (IEP).

---

7 Alternative ways of communicating without verbal speech, often using technology.

8 www.makaton.org

9 www.talkingmats.com

3. **Portable symbol based communication systems e.g. PECS,**[10] **Communicate in Print,**[11] **and BOARDMAKER**[12] – Where a young person is able to recognise symbols, carrying these on a portable Keychain can be a very useful way of using visual supports for young people who struggle to process spoken communication, especially at periods of high anxiety. These systems can also be used as the basis for a whole range of visual supports.

4. **Speech generating devices (SGDs) or voice output communication aids (VOCA)** – These are electronic AAC systems used to add to or replace speech or writing. One of these is used by Dr Stephen Hawking, but there is a huge variety of input and display methods including some like Proloquo2Go[13] are available through the Apple App Store on iOS. Some autistic people, even though they can speak well and fluently, find symbol based communication really helpful.

As well as all of these communication devices, one of the best ways to discover how a person is simply to watch them carefully, observe their behaviour, physical posture or whether they make any particular vocalisations and noises that you know that they only make when they're happy. Most of our kids are brilliant at letting us know whether they are happy or not with something that you are doing! If you're seeing lots of behaviours that you don't want, whether of the routine stroppy teenager variety or of a more complex profile such as flapping, tapping, head banging or biting for example, then it might be worth doing some work on the way that you communicate with the person in your care. The more you understand them, identify their fears, their worries and what motivates them, the easier it is to meet their needs. So don't forget to watch what they do if left to their own devices because that can often be particularly instructive.

---

10 www.pecs.com

11 www.widgit.com

12 www.mayer-johnson.com/boardmaker-software

13 www.assistiveware.com/product/proloquo2go

Working with schools and settings

All schools are not the same. They are unique organisations that share a number of key factors, but can vary widely in terms of their ethos,[14] resourcing, location and facilities. They are also very different depending on whether they are nurseries, primary or secondary schools. The environment in which a school is set has a huge impact on what it is able to do and what it is able to offer your child. A large inner-city secondary school is unlikely to have the same sports facilities for example as a similarly sized secondary school in a more rural area. When looking for a school for a child with an unusual profile of needs and strengths, bear in mind that the leadership and ethos of the school has a very big impact. Do they have any special teaching or classes? Does the school encourage ALL students, or just ones who get good academic results? I would always choose a school with the right beliefs ahead of one with the right facilities.[15]

Most children will be able to go to a local mainstream school. Just because a child has special needs does not mean that they are not academically able and that they will not be able to do just as well as any other child given an appropriate opportunity. It does, however make matching the setting to the child far more important. You will need the help and support of your child's teachers for them to do well, so you really need to keep relationships with them as positive as you possibly can. Many parents don't want their children labelled, especially when they're moving school, but if a school is unaware of the issues that your child faces and they have hidden disability, the school won't be able to provide them with appropriate support. So ideally, look for somewhere that understands special needs as well as academic performance and is a supportive and flexible environment.

When things go wrong, as they undoubtedly will at some stage, is the time for you to advocate on behalf of your child. To do that effectively you need to really understand them, and to understand how schools work as well. If you're not sure, ask the teacher you're working with what will work within their setting, find out how far they are able to

---

14 The ethos of a school is what it believes, but is shown by how it works with the children in its care.

15 See Chapter 8 to help you know what to look for in a school for your child.

go and help them to understand how to get the best from your child. In my experience no teacher goes to work intending to do a bad job and to make children miserable, so start from the assumption that they want the best for your child and that you can help them do that. The best schools also provide opportunities for family learning and help you to learn and grow as a parent.

Parents deserve happiness too – why your life matters

Sometimes we feel like we don't deserve to be happy. Especially when you haven't lived up to your own standards and haven't been the sort of parent you want to be. Everybody has a bad day from time to time and no one gets everything right all of the time. So why is it that we tend to be much harder on ourselves than we are on our children? Surely we are learning to be parents in just the same way that they are learning to become adults? I owe my children a huge debt of gratitude for making me a better parent and a more loving person. I always say that they are bringing me up beautifully! It makes them laugh, and it honours the shared role that we play in creating fully functioning, thoughtful and reflective members of society. I would much prefer to be a sort of person who never did a mean thing, and never said an unkind word but sadly I'm human and therefore inherently flawed. That doesn't mean for one second that I don't try to be better, just that I acknowledge that I sometimes get it wrong.

I'm particularly proud of the times when I'm being critical of myself, and it is my children who say, "You wouldn't let me say that about myself, so you don't get to say that about you!" I often tell them that I'm modelling imperfection which is of course a job I do incredibly well. This has two main benefits. Firstly that it means I have someone fighting on my side, even when it's not me. Secondly that they understand that we all have times when things go wrong and when we feel negative and down on ourselves in spite of our very best intentions, but that it's okay and it doesn't last forever. Some people might say that it isn't appropriate to share strong or difficult emotions with children, but I feel that a child's emotions are just as strong and real to them and they need to know why people feel how they do. This is doubly important if the child is on the autism spectrum and sensitive to the strength of the emotion without understanding where it comes from or what to do with it. Understanding what it is, naming the emotion and learning how to deal with it is an especially important skill. I am able to do this with my children because I know that they are able to understand and deal with those emotions appropriately, but this isn't the same for everyone. You need to consider carefully what is appropriate for your children.

The only reason we can be safe enough emotionally to go through that together is because we work very hard to create an environment that is generally positive. When we are faced with challenges, we try to think about the problem aloud, look for possible things that we could do differently and talk through the options, so they can get to see a logical thought process, even if it is talking about an emotional situation. The first stage is accepting that we all get things wrong and that behaving badly sometimes doesn't mean that we're not worthy of being loved. It takes a lot of energy to be able to make a positive difference. As someone who struggles with mood, I have noticed that being down saps my energy, my resourcefulness, and my ability to get things done. Whereas, if you're feeling positive and up, your level of resourcefulness in the face of even the most difficult situations is higher. I know that when I took responsibility for my own life, I immediately felt a lot better, had more energy and was able to run a happier, calmer household. As a result my level of productivity went through the roof and I've been able to achieve more.

Managing other parents

One of the problems of having children with disabilities is that it can be really difficult for other people to understand why they are not behaving in the way that they would normally be expected to. I've lost count of the number of times that other parents have said of a child with autism, ADHD, dyspraxia or dyslexia, "No, he can't possibly have that, he looks completely normal." All of these conditions are hidden. You can't tell just by looking at someone. It makes it really hard for other people to understand why your child is behaving in a particular way, and to make the allowances that they would do if the issues were visible. Stephen McGuinness, an adult with autism who also has a son on the spectrum, describes autism as 'falling over in my mind'. If the child was in a wheelchair, you wouldn't ask them to run a hundred metre race on foot, but if the child with autism takes another child's toy because they don't understand the unspoken social rule that says you should take turns or ask first, they will get into trouble. We need to create a culture where difference is accepted and people are less quick to judge by appearances. When you have a child with a hidden disability you have an opportunity to help work towards a more tolerant society which will benefit not only you and your family, but many other people as well.

It can be really tough in the playground, if your child is behaving in an unusual way and every parent around seems to be judging them and you. It is easy to see why some parents avoid that sort of environment wherever possible and hate school events. Sports day is a particular red flag for many of us. Whilst some children are undeniably brilliant at physical activities and this is where they shine, many more children with special educational needs have issues around coordination, teamwork and understanding rules of the games which make it very hard for them to join in happily. Given how clumsy many of our children are, they tend to be the last to be chosen for any team. I have to tell you that standing there at sports day watching your child be the last one to walk slowly over the line having wandered all over the sports field first, feels rather more like a test of endurance for you than a short sprint for them. The happiest sports day one of my children had was when they had to be removed from it to have a music exam.

I really hope that you are surrounded by a group of lovely parents, who support each other through all the challenges that parenting can bring. However there are times and places where that doesn't seem to be the case. It is always worth avoiding on principle anyone whom you know to be highly competitive in terms of how well their child is doing. Whilst you can wish them well and be happy for them, you don't need to put yourself through the inevitable comparisons that they will bring up, that will fail to show your children in any positive light at all. Feel free not to go. This kind of parenting chat is negative, exhausting and depressing for all parents. Give yourself a free hall pass and don't join in. You'll feel much better. Find something you enjoy doing instead and do it. If you have to be at one of those occasions, it's worth being ready to talk about two or three things that your child did that made you laugh with joy, or feel proud about. It will make you feel 10 times better, and will stop you from feeling so defensive, especially if you can laugh about it. Parent's evenings can be particularly difficult, especially if you live in an area that has a selective education system (such as around 11+ exams and secondary school selection time in the UK). For some reason, the system seems to bring out the worst in most parents and I highly recommend being busy as possible elsewhere so you don't go mad obsessing about the issues.

The world outside your home

Try as you might to create the best possible environment within your home, at some stage your child has to go out into the world and learn to negotiate it as best they can using whatever support is necessary. We all have a role to play in sharing a wider awareness of hidden disabilities because only when people know about conditions do they begin to understand and learn to work with people rather than being scared of them. Scared people behave badly. They can't be relied upon to behave as their best selves when they feel under threat (however unjustified that may be) any more than you would. Many of the disability specific charities such as the National Autistic Society for autism, Dyslexia Action for dyslexia amongst many others, do a great job with government and media in terms of campaigning for the rights of people with disabilities, changing public perceptions of what those disabilities are and how they impact on individuals. You can follow them on Facebook and on Twitter, and retweet to your heart's content positive and helpful stories about disabilities.

It is much easier to accept difference when you know somebody who has condition, but the next best thing is to share stories of celebrities and people in the media who have declared their disability. There are brilliant examples such as Richard Branson[16] and Temple Grandin[17]

---

16 Richard Branson is the owner of the Virgin business empire and is one of a number of businessmen who have become very successful entrepreneurs despite struggling at school with dyslexia.

17 Temple Grandin is an adult with autism from the USA who is famous for developing a cruelty-free system of handling cattle in the US that minimises their distress. Read more

who have been hugely successful and provide good examples of what people can achieve.

There is a deep psychological pull towards people who are the same as us whatever that may be. But the world needs us to be different from each other. We need people with different skills, abilities, and ways of seeing things in order to be able to create solutions to the problems that we face as a society or to make art and music that enriches our lives beyond belief. So often, it is people who are unusual who lead the way in the fields of science, engineering, technology, computing, music, theatre and the arts. Just as the planet needs a range of different plants and animals to flourish, mankind needs a range of different people with different physical and mental emotional and spiritual strengths, to illuminate and show us what it means to be human in all its beauty. We need human diversity every bit as much as biodiversity.

Building resilience

There are so many ways in which being different and having additional needs leaves children vulnerable – whether it is not being able to communicate effectively, not understanding when someone is really being a friend and when they are being manipulative. It may be an inability to accept failure. Children are vulnerable to issues with self-esteem, manipulation, abuse, mental health issues and fewer and less rewarding employment opportunities. All of this makes it so much more important that as parents we build their ability to be knocked down and pick themselves back up again. That we give them an unshakeable sense of their value and worth in the world, even if the rest of the world doesn't see it the way that we do.

For anyone to grow, they have to learn to communicate, to express choices, and to deal appropriately with failure. If I can't communicate effectively that I do or don't like something, I'm completely at the mercy of those taking care of me. Yet if someone shows me that communicating makes a difference, and helps me to find a mechanism that works for me, I can begin to choose my life as an individual. Once I am able to make choices, then I need to learn that there will be times when I can choose and times when I cannot.

about her in Chapter 3.

Even people with very high levels of fluency in terms of speaking can really struggle with their need to control and make the world around them predictable. No life goes entirely to plan, so we have to work on developing flexibility of thought and choice within a framework that is respectful of the wishes of the individual as far as is possible. Having the courage to learn means having the courage to fail. This can be a really difficult concept to live with, when you have a very wide perfectionist streak.

To balance out the really important role in providing frustration and challenge in order to help a young person grow, we also need to recognise successes when they happen however small they may be. It helps to focus on what you can do and to look to change, not blame. Success may be making progress, learning something new, or perhaps it's a good day because no one got bitten today! I found it really useful to look for something that went right even in the middle of something that went wrong. This could be a simple as thinking of another way to approach a written exercise, or enjoying a nice walk in the sunshine after a day that was particularly challenging.

If in doubt, think of five things to be grateful for that happened in the last 24 hours. They could be big or small, but remember them in as much detail as you can adding in the sights, sounds, smells, taste or feel of whatever it is you're recalling. I'm a great fan of the glory file where I keep a copy of anything that has gone really well. Include thank you letters, certificates, or even a positive email in the folder. Anything to balance out the bad days.

Worrying about the future

One of the biggest worries of any parent is how their child will cope without them. How they will manage at nursery... big school... secondary school... college... in their own home... after I've gone? Talking to people who have adult children, the issue doesn't go away. This is especially true for people with learning difficulties who aren't able to live independently. Whatever the position of your child, the amount of independence they are able to enjoy depends on your ability and that of the teachers who work with them to develop key abilities throughout their education. It takes many children with special needs much longer to learn life skills than it would children without difficulties, so you have to start earlier and teach them specifically, rather than expecting the child to pick them up along the way.

Worrying on its own is very unproductive. But if you're able to use the fears and concerns that you have to help you plan in a way that avoids the eventualities that worry you, then you're making better use of those thoughts at the same time as protecting your young person in the best way possible. You know your child best, and you will know from your experience of life what issues are likely to provide them with the greatest challenge.[18] You are likely to want to include the following: financial security, education, independence skills, social skills, friendships and relationships, volunteering, work, and special interests. Concentrate on working on those at the same time as building their strengths so that they have productive and enjoyable activities to do once their time in formal education is finished.

The more profound the needs of your young person are, the more robust the support that they will need. If you're fortunate enough to be able to afford to make financial provision for them, then you will be able to specify in far more detail the help that they will get. It's not all about money though; one of the best protections that we can offer vulnerable members of society is to make them a fully functioning member of the community, so that people will look out for them, and take care of them. Often this is best done in the context of work or voluntary activity and it should always be something that adds value and brings joy to their lives.

From surviving to thriving

You have a really hard job as a parent under any circumstances, but the skills, abilities, broadening of outlook and joy that you can experience along the way are uniquely valuable. We are living in a period where there are more sources of support available than ever before. There is no need for you to feel alone in dealing with any issues that you face, but you will have to be active in seeking out people, places and opportunities for you to use for yourself and your child. This book will

---

18 See Chapter 3 for a more detailed discussion of the things to build into your long term plan.

help you to identify the things that you might find helpful, and people who can support you.

Once you've identified your child's strengths and what they might want to do in their future, you can then work backwards to identify the skills, abilities and knowledge they need. Then you can work to find the support that they will require to be able to achieve it. This is all with the full intention of creating with them a life full of joy, a community where they are a valued part and a world that recognises them as a positive influence. Never underestimate how much difference one individual can make. This is your opportunity to do this with your child so that when your time comes to leave them you can do so in peace thinking of your time with them with joy.

Chapter 2

Diagnosis, Acceptance and Moving On

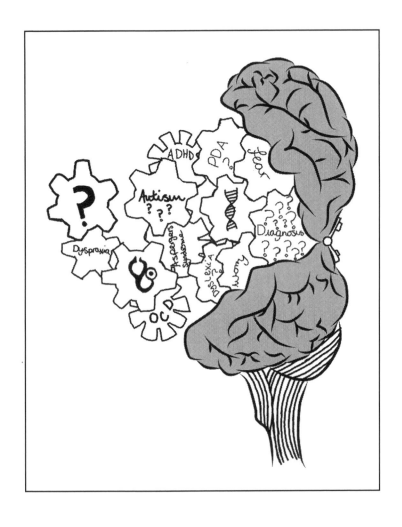

There's something different about my child!

One of the hardest moments in life is that sinking feeling when you realise that everything isn't the way you expected. I am sure that everyone feels it differently, but for me it was a growing realisation that my child wasn't behaving in the same way as other children. I was completely unconvinced and angry at the people who suggested that the beautiful child I saw in front of me wasn't 'normal', whatever that meant. For a long time, it seemed to be just delayed development. In my case the child walked, talked and did the other milestones pretty much on target. As is normal for summer-born children, they did most things later than other members of their year group who were up to nine months older after all.

I went from assuming that the things other people were seeing were mistaken, to thinking that they were right, to wanting to make it better. I saw a future fraught with failures and difficulty. I read terrifying statistics on mental health and suicide rates and I freaked out. For years we tried one thing after another after another to solve our child's 'problem' so they could be 'normal'. All the time we were striving so hard for normal, we were feeling the pain of failure. Again and again we kept rubbing up against expectations that weren't met, both ours and other people's. It was a profoundly upsetting and depressing process. Some things helped, most made no discernible difference. Our child grew and changed. Even now, many of the changes that we have seen we would be inclined in the light of experience to put down to normal development.

As time went by, I started to realise that the gorgeous, wonderful child I had was the same person they always were, no more, no less, and that the issues they face were ones to be dealt with, not wished away. My role in life had changed, and I realised that if I had difficulty with it, that was a problem for me to deal with, not anyone else. I had to realise that it was not my fault, and thinking about fault was really unhelpful. The reality of dealing with a life lived differently took up way too much energy without worrying about causes. My natural reaction is to dive into research. I discovered how many disabilities overlap and uncovered stories of inherent strengths. I looked into the brain differences of a range of disabilities, and slowly began to

23

discover gifts that I had been unaware of. Science moves on and people's understanding of what brain development is changes as time goes by. If you look at a disability as a deficit or lack of something, then it is harder to see the benefits that a condition can bring, whereas looking at it as a 'diffability'[19] or different ability opens up a world of possibilities. We need to look with better eyes.

Where can I go and who can help?

Who can help you will depend on the age of the child at the time. For very young children, a Health Visitor (or Paediatrician in the US) may be the first port of call as they understand what typical development is for the Under 5s. Whether your child is seen as having an issue will depend on whether they meet the normal developmental milestones. There are really useful tools available through the NHS[20] and CDC which you can use to decide if your child is falling behind. Although no two children develop in exactly the same way and at the same time, there are a number of stages that you would expect them to follow at particular ages.

If your child is very severely affected by their condition, it may well have been very obvious from an early stage that something is different, which makes identification easier. It is hard to know what typical development is when you have your first child. Unless you are raised around a lot of babies and very young children, you have no other children to compare them with and they are your picture of normal. For older children, your doctor or GP is usually the first port of call for a developmental referral onto specialist diagnostic services. It is really helpful to prepare a list of the things that are worrying you and why you feel that a referral is necessary.

For many parents, the first indications that they have may be from a member of nursery staff or a teacher, as they see far many more children than you do as a part of their work, so find it easier to spot when something is different. You may well have been referred for

---

19 A term I first heard used by Dr. Wenn Lawson to describe having a different way of seeing and doing things, as an alternative to disability.

20 The NHS have developmental milestones on their website at www.nhs.uk/Tools/Pages/birthtofive.aspx as do the Center for Disease Control in the USA at www.cdc.gov/ncbddd/actearly/milestones/

hearing tests if your child is not responding normally, or has attention problems, as it is important to rule out simple physical issues first. The first indication I had were when my child hid under tables and put their hands over their ears. It turns out that both of them have inherited my sensitivity to sound and they couldn't stand the noise and clashing of nursery school music lesson, but were fascinated by the overlapping sounds of the echo of singing rebounding off the walls in the toilets.

Are there any problems with going for a diagnosis?

My husband worried about getting a diagnosis as if it might turn our child into someone else. He worried about labelling both of our children, that they would not be accepted and that it would marginalise them in society. We both worried that teachers, friends, family, and other people wouldn't see them in the same way. That it would turn them into 'that child'. Even when my many meetings with teachers told me they already were 'that child'. We worry that we might not see them as the same people they are. It feels like being handed the thing you ordered from Amazon, to find that you have been handed a mystery parcel instead of what you thought you ordered.

Once we have a name for the thing we think our child has, our normal parental worries become supercharged we start to obsess about it. Some people might feel that their child has been stolen by it. For me, it was like being handed a pass the parcel with a mystery in each layer. Like someone looking online for their symptoms, we go straight to the worst representations of what the future could be, and we are vulnerable to people who promise to cure the condition and make it disappear. We worry about what the impact might be on the young person we know and love. That fear can change over time. As we learn more, and hear more from people with the condition and their families, the fear can recede and be replaced by a more balanced view. We need to learn the capacity to take on board this new information and come out ready to do what our child needs. As the layers of the parcel unwrap we realise that the people we have are infinitely more beautiful, more interesting and bring us more joy than we dared to imagine.

Layered on top of our fears for our children is our fear for ourselves. The shock that something we hadn't planned for has happened. How

25

do we deal with this? Can I cope? Will it affect how I can work? What will other people think? How will it affect our relationships? Initially, we may be absorbed in our own reactions, but the natural tendency to protect our children soon kicks in and we are uniquely sensitive to what people say about our children in a way that we are not about ourselves. The way that we react is affected by what the label is, what we know and how comfortable we are with the diagnosis and the views that society has of the condition.

Can diagnosis be helpful?

Knowing the nature of what you are facing, how your child thinks, what their natural strengths and weaknesses are is hugely helpful in terms of helping them to thrive. A lot of research has focussed on ways to identify neurological conditions in progressively younger and younger children. The advantage of this is that everything we know suggests that the young brain learns skills and knowledge much quicker than older people. We know that the brain can make new connections and is much more flexible than we once thought. Young people with neurological differences will often need to be taught explicitly how to develop skills which others seem to learn without effort. It takes time, focus and attention, and it really helps to know what to concentrate on. Many professionals recognise the importance of early intervention which is defined as intervention after diagnosis, whenever that occurs. In retrospect, I wish we had gone for an earlier diagnosis with our second child, but we thought that our experience would be as poor with our second child as it was with the first. When we finally went for it, the diagnosis was different and the support on offer was better, but the biggest difference was in our readiness to deal with whatever came up.

Although in theory services are based around need rather than diagnosis, in practice, having a label not only gives access to specialist services, it also helps people to know what approaches are likely to be effective. Given the complexity of many children's presentation and the ongoing pressure on resources, the professionals that you will be relying on to help your child need to short circuit the trial and error process as far as possible. Although the threshold for specialist services does vary from place to place, having a diagnosis is often a gateway to support for you and your child.

I meet lots of people with autism and for two years I asked each and every one, "What two things would have made your life at school better?"

Without exception, they all said that a diagnosis has been essential for them and that it finally explained why they were different, and why they found some things difficult. Next, they wanted to be accepted by society as they are. Having a hidden disability can make it hard for people around to understand why you are behaving in a certain way. For many adults with autism, they say diagnosis is an integral and important part of their identity which brings them comfort and a sense of belonging. This is especially so for many people with Asperger syndrome who have formed identities as 'Aspies' and fought (and failed) to keep the diagnostic label in the American diagnostic manual DSM(V)[21] where Asperger syndrome has been included into autism spectrum disorder (ASD). The Diagnostic and Statistical Manual of Mental Disorders (5th ed.; DSM–5; American Psychiatric Association, 2013) is the most widely accepted nomenclature used by clinicians and researchers in the US for the classification of mental disorders. It is also widely used throughout the world.

Diagnosis – the waiting game

Normally in the UK a child will be referred for specialist assessment by either their doctor (GP) or school. The exact process and pathway varies from place to place. An assessment is usually carried out by a paediatrician, ideally a speech and language therapist and educational psychologist as part of a multi-disciplinary team with input from parents and school. The National Institute for Health and Care Excellence (NICE) has produced guidance on how this should work.[22] Some children make it very easy for professionals to identify their issue because they fall neatly into the diagnostic criteria, or are very severely affected. This makes it easier for parents to explain what is obvious and apparent to anyone seeing their child; the flip side is that their road

---

21   American Psychiatric Association. (2013). *Diagnostic and statistical manual of mental disorders* (5th ed.). Arlington, VA: American Psychiatric Publishing.

22   www.nice.org.uk/guidance/cg128

is an especially hard one. There is no cure for autism. It is a life-long condition.

A child who does not talk can simplify the diagnostic decision, but whose life outcomes are likely to be less rosy, as they may well need life-long support. That is not to say for one minute that they cannot be happy, healthy and live a life with meaning and love, but that they will need thoughtful long-term care to achieve it.

Given that rates of diagnosis continue to increase and resources continue to decrease, it is not surprising that there is huge pressure on diagnostic services, which vary greatly from place to place. So what can you do whilst you are waiting? Find out as much as you can on the conditions that you suspect, but don't scare yourself to death. Television is getting better at covering special needs and disability issues, but bear in mind that they do tend to want to sensationalise the presentation to make it more entertaining for viewers, so are not really a fair reflection of life for most people. Read as much as you can, but make sure that you look at sources that put the individual with the condition at the centre of what they do. First-person accounts are always the best representation of an individual's experience, but again, you do need to bear in mind that it is just one person's experience and your child is a different person.

The best sources are often specialist sources, especially national charities. Start with the 'what is…' information and keep reading for as long as you want. Whether or not what you read applies directly to your child, it may well apply to one of their friends, or someone else you know. Other reliable sources are governmental health bodies like the NHS in the UK. You should be properly suspicious of any organisation offering a cure or treatment in exchange for money. You are particularly vulnerable at this stage and will naturally want to do anything to make life easier for your child. Don't do it without doing your homework first!

Diagnosis, grieving and renewal

Any major life change takes a huge emotional adjustment and learning that you have a child with a disability definitely counts. Many parents speak about the devastation that they have felt when being told that there child has a lifelong neurodevelopmental condition such as autism or dyslexia. This is partly as a result of the poor image of people with disabilities in the media. People I have spoken to have said that it felt like a bomb had gone off in their lives and that their child had changed irrevocably now that they had this label. Although the child is exactly the same on the way out of the room as they were entering it, it does not reduce the impact on the parent the tiniest bit! The strength of your reaction is also conditioned by how much you know, your cultural assumptions, how much support you have and your level of resources. Initially, the shock of hearing the words said can be devastating, and some parents will avoid a diagnosis in the hope of escaping a difficult and painful emotional process.

In some ways, the process of adjustment is very similar to the stages that you go through when someone that you love dies. Although your child is still with you, and especially when they are very young and are severely affected, you may have a picture in your mind of what their future might be, that you now realise might not happen quite how you imagined. Before you are able to get to grips with your new reality, you may feel a tsunami of emotions which have a lot in common with grief. Of course there is nothing that can compare with the grief of losing a child, and I wouldn't want to suggest for one moment that they are the same because they are not. We can be shocked and surprised by what we feel and the strength of our emotions. Any change you have not chosen can be highly challenging to deal with as you have to give up the situation that you thought you had which can feel like a profound loss similar to grief. There are a number of phases[23] that you might go through (see overleaf).

It takes time to work through each of the stages. Rather than moving smoothly into and out of each stage in turn, it is more as if we start dealing with one stage, and will move on, only to revisit it again as if to consolidate what we've learned, before moving on and slowly beginning to feel a growing sense of optimism and possibility. When coming to terms with a major change, everyone's reactions are different

23 Based on the Grief Cycle from Elizabeth Kubler-Ross, Kübler-Ross, E. (2005) *On Grief and Grieving: Finding the Meaning of Grief Through the Five Stages of Loss*, Simon & Schuster Ltd, ISBN 0-7432-6344-8

and highly personal which means that even parents who are very close are unlikely to be at the same stage at the same time.

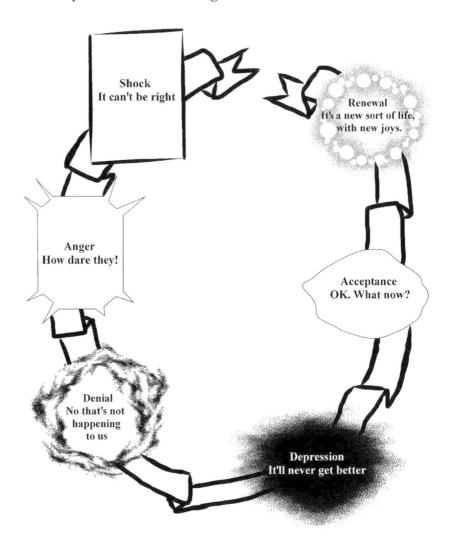

There is absolutely nothing wrong with feeling like this. It is a normal physiological reaction to a shock and it is important for you to allow yourselves time to process what this difference means to you and your family.

The Autism Education Trust has made available a series of short films produced by young people themselves, explaining what receiving and understanding their diagnosis has meant to them.[24]

When you are working through the impact of any major life change, you need to be gentle on yourself. No-one enjoys the process of going through what feels like an endless list of ways in which your child can't do things the way other children do. Going for a diagnosis isn't something you would do unless your child had experienced significant problems in the first place, and those are upsetting enough on their own. So please make sure that you do things that you find helpful and help you to feel cared for yourself whilst all this is going on. Many people ring a disability-specific helpline for more information, support, or a sympathetic listening ear. Do what you love to do, talk to people who are supportive, take time out, eat chocolate, build a shed, go paddling, bake cake, build model trains, do some sport or whatever floats your boat! Some of us like to switch into research mode and find out everything there is to know. That is helpful too. Remember this is just one of those bumps in life's highway and this too will pass. A friend described this feeling as saying that it feels as if it is the defining part of your life at the time, but that later you realise it was just a part of your life. Then you realise, with unexpected gratitude, that you have become someone you would not have been otherwise, and that you like this person better.

Is it my fault, why me?

There is no easy answer to this question and what we know seems to change from day to day. What we do know is that many neurodevelopmental conditions seem to run in families, but that it is not directly controlled just by genetics. It appears that a number of other factors may also be interacting; we have no proof of what those are. We do know for definite that autism is not caused by emotionally cold mothers denying love to their offspring. In other words, IT IS NOT YOUR FAULT! Let me say that again clearly, IT IS NOT YOUR FAULT! You may have a different set of genes, you may live in a less than ideal environment, you may have experienced things in your pregnancy that you hadn't wished for, but I am sure that very few of us

---

24 These individual films by young people can be viewed free online at: http://www. autismeducationtrust.org.uk/resources/diagnosis%20dvd/films%20by%20young%20 people.aspx

would intentionally harm our children even if we knew that we could.

One of the perils of being a parent is watching the TV or listening to the radio to find out that yet another thing that you have done has actively messed up your child. Part of our role as parents is to model the ability to be less than perfect and to live from our mistakes. So if you discover that they are a brittle asthmatic, you might want to give up smoking, but beyond that we just do the best we can and what is good for one child isn't necessarily good for another. We are all feeling our way through uncertainly and by all means change your behaviour when you have new information, but life cannot be lived with joy if you are always lugging guilt around with you. I am reminded of a scene in a film called *The Mission* when a priest heaves a huge net full of metal up a cliff as atonement until it threatens to pull him off the cliff and is cut away by his travelling companion. Sometimes you just have to let things go.

Maybe a better question is 'Why not me?' Do you think for one minute that other people in a similar position to yours deserve to live with this and you do not? In the end, whether you feel guilty or not does nothing except get in the way of doing what you need to for your child. You have challenges enough and it is important to clear your head, your diary and your conscience to deal with those. If you feel stuck, find someone to help you through the issues, whether it is a priest, a counsellor or a friend. Your child needs you to be on their side, batting for them, not beating yourself up. There is a huge strength in finding the good in each and every situation, however difficult it is at the time. Teenager Stephen Sutton[25] when diagnosed with terminal cancer in his 20s, set himself a series of challenges and raised over £2 million for the Teenage Cancer Trust.

Life after diagnosis – what next?

Congratulations! Your child is now the proud owner of one (or more) diagnoses! You have joined an exclusive club of people united by the fact that they don't have to pretend to be 'normal' anymore and can just get on with the far more important business of becoming the person they were born to be. This can be a really positive moment, where you

25 www.teenagecancertrust.org/get-clued-up/young-peoples-stories/stephen-sutton/

and your child can claim the role models that they would like to cite when someone asks 'what is it like to have dyslexia' or whatever your issue might be, you can have a list of the people with that condition who have been hugely successful. Think of people like Richard Branson who is a very successful entrepreneur. There are sites that list people with specific conditions. Find the ones that mean something to your child and use them for encouragement.[26]

What if your child also has a learning disability, is non-verbal, or screams if the street lamp goes off at a different time of day to normal? How on earth can you feel that your child's condition is a winning lottery ticket? Actually, you can't because it isn't. What you do have is a unique person who is just as capable of living with meaning and joy as anyone else if they feel safe and secure and get to enjoy doing what they love. For the vast majority of people, the reality of living with special needs is somewhere in the middle, sometimes awful, sometimes fantastic, but it mostly just is what you have to do day by day to make things a tiny bit better. It is still worth the effort.

Now you have a diagnosis in your hot little hand it is time to go looking for the things that you think will make a difference for your child, whether that is changing what you do at home, specialist teaching after school or a social group for a late-diagnosed teenager. Things change really quickly on what is available, so look to the most current sources for local information. Ask the professional who gave you a diagnosis if there are any local parent groups as they are often the best informed on local resources. Your nursery, school or college may also have specialist support. Ask the SENCO (Special Education Needs Coordinator) or a member of staff in Student Support for their suggestions. Don't forget the mainstream activities that might work well for your child. Shared interests can be the best route into friendships and it is really important that your attention is focussed on what will bring your child joy, not just on how to fix any problem they might have. No-one likes to feel like someone else's pet project especially when they are teenage, when you might inadvertently cause huge resentment.

One of your most important decisions will be who to tell, what to say and how much to say. I would suggest that you make sure you have

---

26 www.dyslexia.com/famous.htm for dyslexia.

come to turns with the diagnosis before you start telling people outside the ambit of Health/Education/Social Care. Telling someone can feel like going through the process of diagnosis all over again as you see the reaction in their eyes. There are safe spaces within which to have this discussion and ones that are more risky in terms of their reaction and how that can make you and your child feel.

Learning from the best

There are people around you who can help provide information and advice (avoiding of course, your own version of Great Aunt Mabel who has her own unique perspective and suggests that all children should be beaten until they behave 'properly'!). If you have a friend whose child has a diagnosis and yours is doing similar things, feel free to talk to them, they might also be glad of someone to talk to who has some idea of what life is like for them. Many specialist disability charities run local branch networks run by volunteers to support parents. Don't be afraid to approach them if there is one in your area. If there isn't, you might like to think about setting one up. Many people find exchanging your stories from parenting on the front line particularly helpful. Don't forget that your school may well have parenting courses, parents groups or prayer groups which can be a good source of support.

Look for books on your child's condition. Check the reviews to see whether people find them helpful, and look at the author biography to make sure that the author knows their stuff. There are a limited number of people at the absolute top of their game in any one subject, so don't forget to learn from the best. I don't think you can authentically understand what it is like to have a condition without listening to people who have it. Some of the most powerful books, blogs and training come from autistic people such as Temple Grandin, Kamran Naseer and Luke Jackson. Go and read them; they are fascinating in their own right although by their very nature these do tend to reflect the experience of people who are verbal and of at least average intelligence. What they do not represent is people who use augmented and alternative communication (AAC), or other people with learning difficulties. It is especially worth looking at *The Reason Why I Jump* translated by David Mitchell as one of the few books that represents this part of the autism spectrum.

I have found that attending training and conferences run by charities or parents groups is one of the best ways to get a thorough understanding of the condition, and it does give you the opportunity to talk to other people. Look for 'events' on the internet to find them. The real strength of these events is that they usually cover quite a range of issues, giving you a wider perspective.

Telling your child

Deciding if and when to tell your child is not an easy decision to make for many people, and much will depend on the child themselves, their age and ability to understand what it means. Although many people would suggest that a non-verbal person does not need to know about the details, I would argue that they do need to be able to convey what they do and don't like and what they need in order to feel safe. Tony Attwood[27] suggests that young people describe themselves as 'I am someone who…' rather than 'I have Asperger syndrome'.

There is a host of materials for people of all ages that are very accepting of difference, although many of them are available through specialist Special Needs publishers, such as Jessica Kingsley.[28] Books for and by teenagers, such as *The Asperkid's (Secret) Book of Social Rules*[29] by Jennifer Cook O'Toole and *Martian in the Playground*[30] by Claire Sainsbury or *Freaks, Geeks and Asperger Syndrome*[31] by Luke Jackson are all helpful in reinforcing the positives of being different. Many young people find that particularly helpful. I would always recommend finding appropriate and positive role models for the particular disability that your child has. There is real joy in knowing about people with your

---

27 Tony Attwood. *The Complete Guide to Asperger Syndrome*. London: Jessica Kingsley, 2008. ISBN-10:1843106698

28 http://www.jkp.com

29 Jennifer Cook O'Toole. *The Asperkid's (Secret) Book of Social Rules: The Handbook of Not-so-obvious Social Guidelines for Tweens and Teens With Asperger Syndrome* Paperback. London: Jessica Kingsley. 2012. ISBN-10: 1849059152

30 Clare Sainsbury. *Martian in the Playground: Understanding the Schoolchild with Asperger's Syndrome* Lucky Duck Books, 2009.

31 Luke Jackson. *Freaks, Geeks & Asperger Syndrome: A User Guide to Adolescence*, London: Jessica Kingsley, 2002.

condition and it can be a real spur for success. Although I am less convinced about assigning current diagnoses to historical figures, there are many people living who have shared their diagnoses. It is worth looking online to find ones that you know your child will identify with such as Disabled World[32] which has long lists of people with specific disabilities.

You are likely to need to explicitly teach them what to say in different scenarios as lots of our children are socially naïve and will not have the most positive way of phrasing what they know. Some parents have chosen not to tell their young person in order to protect them. The young people I have come into contact with have all been aware of their diagnosis. If your choice is not to say anything about it to your child because you think it will make them stand out, it seems likely that they already stand out. Not disclosing their diagnosis to them risks leaving them isolated and unsupported, which can only increase their vulnerability. It also runs the risk of them feeling that it is something to be ashamed of rather than celebrated.

New ideas, new friends

Even the most positive person tends to feel that living with a child who is not 'normal' has cast a cloud over your life from time to time. You wouldn't be human if you didn't want life to be easy from time to time. Let's put aside for the moment the thought that what is 'normal' is definitely open to discussion, and think about what that cloud actually means. Without clouds we would have no rain, without rain there would be no growth and therefore no life. Everyone has things they didn't ask for land in their lives. Not all of these things are good, but there is always something positive that can come out of them. Some people tend to be more positive, others more negative, but this is something that you can change if you choose to.

So how do you do that? It is first and foremost a decision. You need to decide that there are important things that you can learn as a parent and as a human being through what you are experiencing. For many of us, it is learning to look at our children in a deeper and more loving way. Having been forced out of life in the smug zone where everything just trots along without us having to do much, we are forced to stop and pay attention. But before you get the idea that this only applies to parents of children with special needs, you might like to attend any parenting class up and down the country. They are full of people like us who just need to collect a different set of ideas and learn some new skills because what they have in their personal toolkit isn't enough, or isn't working! These are great people to surround yourself with because they are in a similar situation to you. When you are really struggling, the last thing you need is to spend time with the friend whose children are always high achieving, never get anything wrong, have perfectly tidy rooms, clean up after themselves, only speak respectfully and never make mistakes. Oh hang on a minute! I can't think of anyone like that, can you? I do know people who tell you that is so. You know it isn't the whole of the story, but we don't always want the things that hurt us most and make us question ourselves on show to the world.

Whatever life will be for you and your child, it will not be boring! New challenges are thrown at us daily, we come up with solutions and then need to find the solution to the next challenge. There is a blessing in the excavation work that you may well need to do to identify what your child's skills are. Some may be completely obvious, like Stephen Wiltshire's amazing ability to draw an entire city scape in incredible detail, having seen it just once. Others are much harder to find. Like the ability of a non-verbal child to paint in a way that captures a different view of the everyday. The vast majority of skills that we and our children develop are the result of hour upon hour of effort. What many people mistake for genius is often just the result of repeated and persistent effort. The autistic child's attention to detail brings a real strength here. Or the restless energy of the ADHD child which enables them to keep going long after lower energy people have given up and gone for a lie down!

Snake oil and real help – how to tell the difference

It is perfectly natural for any parent to want to help if their child is in pain, in difficulty or deeply unhappy. We just want it to stop and may turn to a range of medicines, therapies and interventions to find something that can help. This is completely natural and is a good impulse. The problem comes when you are trying to correct something that is an inherent part of the person. Nowadays, we wouldn't beat a child for writing with their left hand, although there are still people within living memory who were. In the same way, there are passionate advocates for autism rights for example who say that their autism is a hugely important part of their identity. That it isn't something that they suffer from; although it may bring difficulties, it is part of who they are. Their motto is nothing about us without us.[33]

If your instinct is to place your child at the centre of your plans, and use their strengths to build their skills, then I feel that you are moving in the right direction. The problem with discovering that your child is different is that in your protectiveness you are desperate to make life easier. It leaves you very vulnerable to people and organisations that are looking to make money out of your natural instincts. What we do know about these conditions is that there is a neurological difference. The brain is wired differently. Not wrong, just different. How likely is it then that a fundamental difference can be 'cured'? I have no doubt that children can learn to use their skills differently and can develop, but our experience to date leads us to believe that a cure is neither possible, nor is it desirable. Although there are now a handful of children who apparently no longer meet diagnostic criteria,[34] I find it unlikely that their inherent wiring has been changed even if their functioning ability has, and I worry about the long term implications of them not being ok unless they are 'cured'. There is a generation of older people with autism who were not diagnosed as children, and substantial numbers speak passionately about the pain of having to fit in and to pass as being 'normal'. Without the skills that people who think differently bring, we have no innovation, no development, and the world always has need of the unique skills that divergent thinkers bring. Whether their perceptual style is different as a result of autism, ADHD or any other condition, we need diversity, not monoculture.

---

33 Disability rights author, James Charlton relates that he first heard the term used in talks by South African disability activists Michael Masutha and William Rowland and used the phrase.

34 As reported in the New York Times article The Kids Who Beat Autism by Ruth Padawer July 31, 2014.

What do we know that helps? Well, we know that the younger you start learning anything, the more plastic, malleable and changeable a child's brain is. So teaching children things that they might find difficult early is a great way to make the most of this golden period. Does it mean that if you get a late diagnosis it is too late? No, of course not, just that learning may take a little longer. Be aware when looking at findings that there are a number of indicators to judge the strength of research:

1. **Who is paying for it?** Is there a vested interest that needs to reinforce a specific outcome?

2. **What is the size of the sample?** Single cases are anecdotal stories, not proven interventions. The bigger the numbers involved, the better.

3. **Has the study been replicated by other people?** Although new research always has to be done by a single group, it doesn't become proven unless the studies have been repeated by other groups in other places.

4. **Was it a 'double-blind' randomised control study or Randomised Control Trial (RCS/RCT)?** RCS/RCTs are the research 'gold standard'. This is where the people within a study are assigned to two groups at random. One group receives the treatment or intervention, the other receives nothing, or a placebo (a sugar pill that contains no active ingredients). A double-blind study is where neither the individuals, nor the people carrying out the tests know which patient is in which group, avoiding any bias in the observer.

5. **What is the population selected, and how well does this match the position you and your child are in?** The results that you get are highly dependent on who is included in the first place.

6. **Observer bias** – If, as a parent, you pay for an intervention or have invested your emotion and time in it, you are far more likely to assume that any changes in the development that you see are as a result of what you have paid for, when they may simply be developmental, or may be caused by something else altogether!

What if I can't find what my child needs?

You are the person who knows your child best. If you believe they need something you can't find locally you will have to find a way of them getting what they need. The only rider I would add to that is that your ability to be able to assess accurately what might be available will be helped no end if you take help, advice and guidance from as many people as possible who know and have contact with your child. Remember that you have the right to discount or ignore that advice in the best interests of your child. I have often heard professionals say that parents can be overprotective and so don't give them as much chance to develop as typically developing children. Whilst this is completely understandable, as parents we have to learn every day how to let our people grow into the best versions of themselves that they can become. This means sometimes allowing them to experience, frustration, fear, new things and challenge. Ros Blackburn, an adult with autism said that is has been important for her parents to challenge her and push her to do things she doesn't want to do.

In 1962, a small group of parents in the UK sat around a kitchen table who were unhappy with the institutionalised future that was on offer for their children. That day a group of friends set up the National Autistic Society. In the first 50 years it has set up 6 schools to educate young people with autism and campaigned for the rights of people with autism to live the lives that they choose. Their tireless campaigning led to the first ever disability-specific legislation in the Autism Act. This pattern has been replicated in much of the charity sector. Many organisations are started by highly committed and motivated parents who see that there is a need that is not being satisfied. They become the change they want to see.

So how can you do this? Not everyone has the time or money to be able to set something up from scratch, nor should you if there is already something out there already that you can use. Look around to see what organisations can help you. Many organisations have been set up by parents for parents. If they are close enough to what you need for you or for your child, use them. Many parents have told me that there isn't enough help locally for them; although branches exist, they are a long way away from where they live. It is not difficult to set up a branch.

Most organisations have support at the centre of the charity to help, but what people need most is you! Your experience, your passion for your child and your care is all that is needed to set something up. This group may well help you through some rough times of your own. Don't forget the online groups too. They are accessible to people whatever hours they are working and irrespective of where you are based.

Chapter 3

Know Your Child

Information is power

If you have a child with Special Needs you need to become the expert in them, their development, their condition, diagnosis, likes and dislikes and everything about them. That may sound like a lot. It is. The good news is that you probably have most of the information that you need to be able to champion, advocate and get the best for your child that you possibly can. You might find it harder to manage how best to keep that information, what you need for specialist assessments and so on. It is really helpful if you have a folder with all of your child's information in one place to take to meetings with teachers and schools so that you can discuss your child in detail and be right on top of their information. I have an A4 folder for each of my children with a copy of every report ever written, and all of the forms I have submitted by date, so that I can refer to them whenever necessary. It was especially useful when going for diagnosis to look through the story that the documents told to build up a picture over time to enhance and back up my own recollections with professional testimony.

What information do you need?

I have noticed that we rarely start out being aware of what might be helpful, or indeed necessary when going for diagnosis or applying for additional support either through your child's school, or with a funding authority such as a Local Authority or School Board. The vast majority of conditions need the diagnostic professionals to take a detailed case history about what your child was like when they were young. Now if you are dealing with an 18 month old-child, that is so much easier than trying to remember that far back when your child is 10 or even if they are seeking a diagnosis as an adult.

If you have them available these are all helpful:

1. **Child development information** – In the UK when my children were small we were given red books to measure the babies' development, but tend not to use them for anything other than developmental checks and vaccination records.

2. **School Reports** – collect academic measures of progress over time – make sure that whenever you get a piece of information

from the school, your record is dated (even if theirs isn't!) so that you can plot your child's progression over time and whether a child is making the progress that would be expected at their age and stage.

3. **Specialist Assessment Reports** – There are a host of these, and which you have will depend on which condition your child is being assessed for. You will need to complete Parent's questionnaires, the school will often complete a schools version and they will form a part of the assessment, along with any tests carried out by an Educational Psychologist, Speech and Language Therapist, Occupational Therapist or other Professional. Keep all of them, they give you a more complete picture.

4. **Log of incidents (at School or outside)** – Many children with Special Needs are especially vulnerable to bullying. Whilst you will hope that any incident is a one-off, if it happens more than twice, you should start keeping a log of the date, the name of all of the people involved, what your child did and any action you took.

Keeping track of successes

Let's be honest. Life is hard for children with special needs and it is hard for you too. Many children struggle with their levels of self-esteem, whether they are struggling academically, with literacy skills or relationships with other children. One of the most useful things that I ever did was to get one of my children to put together an A4 folder of their own, with a cover showing things that they love. Inside, they put information on the things that they are good at. Every participation certificate, positive comments, online game achievement certificates (the Lego website is particularly good at providing these for their online games). Collect certificates from summer clubs and pictures of your child in uniform with all the badges they have earned in the Scouts, Guides or similar organisations. If they have to move up to a different section and start collecting badges all over again sew their old badges onto their camp blanket. When your child is having a rough day bring out the folder to remind them of their successes.

You might like to keep your own parallel version to keep you positive. Whenever you notice something good, take a photo of it on your phone and print it out for their file. I remember feeling that I had never seen so many smiley stamps on my child's book at one point in junior school, so I counted them up. "Wow, you have 15 smiley faces" sounds so much better than "That book was good." Add photos of times and places where you and your child have been happy and hang them round the house.

Use the strengths they have to help you feel good about things. Stick certificates up on the wall, and stick up pictures that they have done that you like. Have a gallery of success looking back at you every day, and change it as often as you have something new to celebrate. If, like many families, it feels like a drought between moments of success, make smaller goals and document them with photos that you can print out and display.

What is a special interest?

Everyone has things that they like to do, find interesting or compelling. Just think of the people who spend all of their time looking at, reading about, or learning how to do, use, or become something related to a special interest. From time to time, TV programmes appear showing a person with a passion for collecting (usually in the context of 'Help! it is taking over the house!'). Their passion is sometimes popular, like someone who collects Star Wars memorabilia or Transformers and sometimes rather more niche, such as an interest in Otis elevators, or escalators.

I have known people to have interests in a huge range of things. Common special interests for young children (especially boys) are Thomas the Tank Engine and Dinosaurs. Doctor Who has been highly popular for generations of fans and is often a special interest across the age range as are other TV shows. Adults might collect airline sick bags (unused!) or antique swords from the Napoleonic era. Teenagers have particular games they enjoy, and some become part of a devoted fan base for online web-based comics like Homestuck which has millions of followers online. What is common to all of these is an all-consuming approach to the subject. Someone with a special interest will read every book, watch every programme, and sometimes travel thousands of miles for their passion.

Is it an obsession? Well, what's in a word? It can certainly look like that to someone who doesn't share the same interest. Put a couple of hard-core Doctor Who fans together at a Comics Convention, surround them with people dressed up as their favourite characters and it looks less strange. A teenager was at a comedy concert, and thought that someone's behaviour was like an Anime character in a title she followed, called out the name of the character, and found someone in the row in front of her turned round, they struck up an immediate conversation, hugged each other and had a great time. "I have found my Tribe," she said joyfully! For a child who spends so much time feeling isolated and alone, finding friends in fandom can provide a sense of belonging they don't get anywhere else.

How can a special interest be useful to you as a parent?

Life and school can be hard for young people who are different – whether as a result of a visible disability or because their behaviour is 'odd' or 'just not what other children do'. It may be that they are interested in different things and cannot see for one moment why the normal concerns of other children are of any interest at all. Whilst most adults are happy to have their own passions and decide what they want to do for themselves, for teenagers it is a time where most children will do almost anything to belong to the group. If the group rejects you, or you were never in it, then life can be very lonely.

Many autistic people will develop a job or career from their special interest. It can bring them great joy. How many of us get to say that? This has a number of advantages. Your young person will be more motivated to do the work necessary to do the job thoroughly. There are many scientists leading the way today whose all-consuming passion for their subject drove them through obstacle after obstacle to deliver significant breakthroughs. Few people who really excel at their subject, or who are at the top of their game are tempted by the parade of possible activities that distracts the rest of us. Olympic swimmers' performance is driven by single-minded determination to succeed backed up by hour upon hour of practice. In *Bounce*[35] Matthew Syed shows that excellence is driven mostly through consistent repetition. Tiger Woods didn't get that good at golf by natural talent alone. He practiced hour after hour, day after day, in all weathers, for years.

Another fantastic benefit of a special interest is that it can be used as a motivator, to persuade your child to do something they wouldn't otherwise want to do. If/then is very powerful! Why should they tidy their bedroom, for example, when it is so boring? If they are given the chance to do something to do with their special interest as a result, then all of a sudden, the boring thing is worth doing. In our household, Saturdays have special significance as they are 3-film Saturday, where the boy gets to choose 3 films on YouTube (his special interest) to show me. This has become a very special time for us, where we have breakfast in bed and I get to keep in touch with the things he is watching. At one stage I was despairing of his ability to tidy his room, so warned him on Wednesday, Thursday and Friday that IF his room was tidy, THEN we could have 3-film Saturday. I was really looking forward to it, but if his room was untidy, 3-film Saturday wouldn't happen. Sure enough, on Saturday morning it was a mess, so I stuck to my guns and said that 3-film Saturday couldn't happen until it was sorted! Cue much wailing and gnashing of teeth, loud protests, throwing of things around the room etc. An hour later he came in and asked for a room inspection. I picked him up on a couple of things, but not before he had been praised for doing a really great job. When those were done, he got 4-film Saturday (an extra choice) as I was so delighted with what he'd done.

What's in the special interest for your child?

Joy – I am sure we have all experienced the complete joy of being so involved in something that the outside world goes away. Whilst many men love their football or other sport, others are equally passionate about their cars, collecting things, or trainspotting. Others of us like to sing, sew, cook, knit, read, bake or do any one of a number of leisure

---

35 *Bounce: The Myth of Talent and the Power of Practice* Paperback – 28 Apr 2011 by Matthew Syed

activities. Whatever it is, the reason why we do these things is because they bring us pleasure. It is no different for our children. Whilst some may find refuge in looking at the night sky and studying the stars, others can find a universe of fascination in reflections of light from a shiny object, the patterns of shadows on the ground or the feel of soft fabric between their fingers.

Safety – When the work outside is scary and unpredictable, going back to the familiar creates a sense of safety and can calm a child who is feeling overwrought. Like Maria in *The Sound of Music* we need our 'favourite things' when feel afraid. Few special interests chosen by children with autism include interaction with other people, which makes the special interest a calm, safe space to be away from social pressures.

Friendships – The vast majority of us need to have some time with people to satisfy the human need for belonging and to feel a part of the world they are in. This is NOT ALWAYS the case with autistic people, some of whom do not want or need to be with other people. Whilst, as in all things, it completely depends on the person, others would like to have social time, but it is so difficult and unpredictable to manage that it is exhausting and they need quiet 'alone' time to de-stress afterwards. As in many things in life, our ability to cope is affected hugely by how much interest we have in what is happening. Being in a small group of people who share your special interest is both easier (no need for small talk) and less stressful as they recognise and respond to the things you love.

Their obsession is driving me mad – how can I manage it?

The first and most important question is, do you need to manage it? If it is not dangerous, not harmful and not taking over to the point that the person doesn't engage with any other activity, then why would you want to take away time with the things that someone loves? I know that I would hate anyone else to tell me I couldn't spend time with someone or something that I love. If it is winding you up, ask yourself whose problem is this? Are you just fed up to the back teeth of talking about Lego, Football, people on YouTube, celebrities, Otis lift systems etc.? (Insert your child's special interest here). Understanding what the special need does for your child makes it much easier to see the value in it. So if the interest doesn't hurt anyone, and is the thing they love to do in your free time – well, go for it!

Having said that, there is a real art in life in balancing the things we love with the things we need to do, whether for our financial, emotional, physical, or psychological benefit. Sometimes, much as your young person loves a thing, you do know that they need to actually get up for school, rather than sitting on the bed with one sock on, headphones on and a book/games console/laptop/Lego model in their hand! Your role as a parent is to take the long view from where they are now and what they can do, towards where they could be in the future and build the path from here to there.

To do that, you need to use all the things you know about your child, what they love to do, their strengths and weaknesses. Unlike your child, you have a lived experience that gives you the ability to see what might work for them. But here comes a bit of a warning; we only know about our own life, those close to us and those who we have heard about, the things that 'people do'. When your child is different from other people, you need to think differently about what this might mean for their future. Pay absolutely no attention to anyone who says, "Of course, they will never…" History is littered with people who were told that they would never amount to anything because they were 'failing' at school and didn't do things the same way as everyone else. Bill Gates dropped out of college, is he a failure? Einstein didn't speak until he was 5, was he a failure? Edison failed 99 times to create the electric filament light bulb, until his persistence found a way that did work. Don't give up! All of those examples are of people who did what they love and persisted until it became a success.

Special interests and school

The fantastic thing about special interests is that it is possible to help a young person to learn what they need to learn if you use their special interest to key them into the subject. It can stretch the creativity of a teacher, but it can be a liberating process for both parties. So if your 5 year old son is passionately interested in dinosaurs, they can be used to teach a lot of the curriculum. Some examples to get you thinking are listed below:

- **Maths** – Counting dinosaurs. How many Diplodocus in the herd? If a Tyrannosaurus Rex eats 1 Triceratops a week, how many would he need to kill in 2 weeks, 4 weeks?

- **English** – Write a story about a dinosaur or report on a school visit to the Natural History Museum.

- **Geography** – Where have dinosaurs been found?

- **All about Me** – Eyes, ears and size – yours in comparison to the dinosaur's?

The main thing is to make it relevant to them and make it fun. Most children will learn so much more when they see the subject is relevant to them because it is something they are interested in. Step into their world and travel with them in it. You will understand them, their perspectives and their strengths so much better as a result.

Teachers are a hugely resourceful bunch. They spend much of their day trying to marry together their subject with the variable and varying interests and attention span of the children that they have in their class. Be under no illusion, what you are asking them to do is extra work. But, it is work that will unlock the ability of a child to learn, respond to them and the subject they need to teach, and for most teachers, that moment of getting through to a child, when they have a moment when they really crack a part of a subject is what they came into teaching for.

Championing your child

Ok, this is really hard to get right. As a parent, it is so, so difficult not to be defensive about your child, especially when the person in front of you is telling you something you really don't want to hear about what your child is or isn't doing. This is why it is all the more important that you work out a way of fighting for your child without fighting the people who are in a position to help.

- **Set positive expectations for the relationship between you and the person you are trying to work with** – At least start off assuming that they are trying to help, but that you may not be looking at things from the same point of view.

- **Focus on the child and state your common aim – What are you both trying to achieve?** What can you both contribute and how can you help to make it easier for them to do what your child needs? Yes, I know you are exhausted, and this does feel like one job too many for you, but at least try to approach them from this point of view and you are far more likely to win an ally. Even if they are not likely to agree, you can usually get someone to agree that the wellbeing of the child is the common area that you are both working towards.

- **Sell the benefits of what you want to happen** – Do you want to use a special interest to unlock a child's potential, try alternative literacy strategies at home and school, or set in place a consistent behaviour management plan? People are always better motivated if they can see a positive outcome. If you are fortunate enough to have a child who is bright, use their potential to deliver good school results. This will impact on the school and on teachers. If your child's behaviour is challenging to a school, work with them to identify what is causing the behaviour, what it communicates and how to minimise any incidents by providing other means, mechanisms and ways to communicate. You could even offer to write up any positive change that they made for schools inspectors.

- **Stay cool** – If you lose your calm, bring it back by reducing the interaction. Say less, breathe more. If that feels impossible, agree another time to talk if you feel too heated.

- **Learn how to vent your frustration** – Offload your anger with a relative or trusted friend away from the situation. Just don't forget to warn them that this is something that you need to do, and that you aren't cross with them.

Building bridges and finding common ground

It can be very isolating to live with a child whose additional needs may put them at odds with their peer group, teachers and people in the wider society. Most of us all need to feel some sense of belonging, and many of our children are not like their peer group in that they will not get that from a group of similarly aged children. As a parent, this means that you may well be the one in the playground at pick up whose child doesn't run out with their friend. You hear talk of parties and invitations for children around you, but your child is not invited. This is hard to live with.

It is especially important for your well-being and that of your child, that you are able to find things that you can share. This does not depend on whether your child can speak, write, or do any of the things that other children do. It is far more to do with whether you can get yourself into your child's head. To put yourself into their position and to see what they can see. John Williams, a blogger and father of 'The Boy' tells a wonderful tale of a trip on the Docklands Light Railway, where the driverless train becomes a magic carpet, where a toy steering wheel puts them in charge of the train and where for a moment, they achieve pure joy in sharing the moment.[36] That is the best part of parenthood, and whether it is watching the look on your child's face as they are immersed in what they love, or watching them do some small thing you thought they would never achieve, it is that joy that you need to capture, and bottle like a small swarm of fireflies to light your way through the darker days.

You need to do this again, and again, and again. Set times and occasions that you know will bring you both joy. Sometimes these can be very small things or they could be a major day out. You might enjoy 3-film Saturday, building Lego, playing computer games together, Family games night, reading stories, listening to talking books on long journeys or any number of things all give us common experiences to talk to each other about.

If they find things hard at school and with other children, many children develop issues with their confidence and self-esteem – especially as they become older and are able to notice the difference between where they are in comparison to their peers. It is especially acute with children who are able to observe and see what the differences are, but lack the skills and abilities to put it right and they keep getting it wrong time

---

36 Have a look at John's blogs at www.mysonsnotrainman.com

after time. As a result, what they really need is for you to acknowledge what is going wrong, but be relentlessly positive about anything that they do well in order to balance out the painful stuff. Few of us would be happy if the only information we got day after day was negative. So look for any means of identifying anything that went well, or positive experiences. Make sure you use lots and lots of praise. If praise doesn't work for your child, find out what does work and do it often.

A passion can lead to a career

Many children living with neurodiversity have uneven areas of strengths and weaknesses, sometimes referred to as a 'spiky profile'. We all deserve to do something for a living that engages us and enables us to develop in some way. As a result, it is especially important to identify the child's strengths and to look at how these may be harnessed, not just to find ways of helping them to learn, but to find the passion in their life that might be able to give them work if they are capable of doing so. It can sometimes be the key to a profitable, satisfying and effective career.

It makes a huge difference to your child's learning if they get to do things that they are interested in. Many of our youngsters have an almost encyclopaedic knowledge of their special interests. This can be the gateway to a future career. They will notice things related to what they love, will find opportunities, friends and ideally even mentors who will help to share information and time with them. This is not only good for their development socially, but it can give them access to a range of opportunities they might otherwise have missed. A love for a subject can keep people on task long after others would have stopped.

This passion can be used to bolster their strengths, give them access to social opportunities that would not happen otherwise, and is hugely helpful in providing the enthusiasm and drive to get a youngster to do things that they would not have considered or found possible otherwise. Many teachers find it really frustrating when a child can do things like writing about their special interest, but ask them to use the same skills in an area they hate and the skill will disappear as if it had never been there in the first place.

Temple Grandin's story

Temple Grandin is possibly the most famous autistic person in the world. She didn't talk until she was three and a half years old and was diagnosed with autism in 1950. She communicated her frustration by screaming, peeping and humming. If you haven't seen it, I highly recommend the film of her life, *Temple Grandin* starring Clare Danes. It shows how she struggled to communicate with the outside world, how scary a place it was for her, and how important a single teacher had been for her. Without the actions of her mother who made her engage formally in social activities such as helping out at parties, she says that she would not have been able to learn. What was, for her mother, an instinctive response, worked because it provided a structure, a role and a purpose for that social interaction and therefore removed some of the anxiety that was involved in it.

Temple has shared with the world the importance of sensory issues in understanding how she experiences the world and in making it a safe place. Although she cannot tolerate light touch, she found that deep pressure had a very calming effect on her, which led to her developing her own 'squeezing box'. This gave her a sense of where her body is and allowed her to function better. It was this insight and her love for animals on the family farm that has led to a number of developments adopted across the beef industry in the United States and across the world. Most farms now own a cattle crush which holds an animal still and calm whilst they can be worked with by a vet for vaccinations etc.

It is her attention to the patterns of movement in cattle that led to a revolution in the management of slaughterhouses, bringing about more humane ways of handling animals on their route to slaughter, reducing animal distress and improving the quality of the meat. She says, "Parents get so worried about the deficits that they don't build up the strengths, but those skills could turn into a job."[37]

Special interests and motivation

So can a special interest ever be a negative thing? Well, it all depends on what it is and what purpose it serves for the individual. With all

---

37 Have a look at her website at www.templegrandin.com

special interests, there is a risk that the person will spend all of their time engaged in their special interest to the detriment of their general development. Much depends on how they are following it and what it means. So, if Temple Grandin had spent all of her time in the cattle shed and never been drawn out into the social world, or encouraged by her teacher, she would not have developed the ability to communicate so powerfully in writing and in person. Would she have worked so hard to try to communicate if it was not desperately important to her interest in the welfare of animals? Possibly not. We cannot leave children entirely to their own devices if they are to learn, develop and grow.

If you saw a typically developing child doing something that was or could become dangerous to themselves or others, you would not leave them to get on with it, either. Although this is very rare, if a special interest could be harmful to them or others we have to gently steer their interest in a more positive direction. What we can do, though, is to teach them what they need to know by using what they are interested in. Many people's special interests will change over time and without experiencing the fullest possible range of opportunities, it is hard for anyone to find their true passion in life. The best thing to do is diversify wherever possible, use their current special interest to extend into other areas if necessary and redirect them into more constructive channels.

Your main criteria for deciding if a special interest is a problem comes down to 3 simple questions:

1. Is it legal?
2. Will it make my child vulnerable?
3. Will they be safe?

If your answers to any of these questions worry you, then you will need to think of a strategy to develop their interest into other areas. This might mean that you have to look very carefully at what they are getting from the interest and find something similar that they will find satisfying, but without the risk you have identified. If in doubt, get professional help.

So what about the dreaded video games debate? Given all that we know about how impressionable we are to visual stimulus and how engaging some of the current first person Role Playing games are, I personally would not knowingly allow a first person shooter game across the threshold. We are all heavily affected by what we focus on, so why would you encourage your child to focus on negative, violent presentations of a pseudo-reality for children who have difficulty in understanding and interpreting the social rules. If it is OK to swear and be violent in a game, why should that not be OK in the street? If you have already come across this issue, they are older or playing without your permission, then the only thing left for you to do is to actively teach the rules – that role playing behaviour in a game is not acceptable behaviour in the real world. Most people on the spectrum are very rule abiding and respond well to clear guidelines.

Discovering what your child loves

For some children this is so easy that you will be laughing at the thought that you might need to work to find this out. They may talk incessantly of nothing but Dinosaurs, sleep under a dinosaur duvet and have a shelf full of books detailing all aspects of dinosaur life. In which case, congratulations, you are off to a flying start! But what if your child is pre-verbal (or is a teenager) and doesn't use speech much. Well then your powers of detection will swing into action. The best place to start is by watching what they do.

- What do they spend time doing when undirected?

- Watch how they interact with it.

- How much time do they spend on doing it?

- What is it about that activity that they do which captivates their attention?

- What skills are they using in doing/watching/interacting with that?

- Does it tie in with something they are good at?

- Are they creating/developing what they are using, or is it a passive activity?

- Does it calm them, or make them excited?

It is almost impossible to cover interests without referring to sensory issues. Much of what your child does may relate to their profile of sensory needs. They might be sensory seeking, or sensory avoiding and they will naturally gravitate towards activities and places that meet their needs and away from ones that cause them distress. If they spend all of their time plugged into headphones, is that because they love music and are listening actively to the intricacies of harmony and rhythm, or because it protects them from having to talk to other people? Or because having earphones reduces the assault of the noises outside to a level where they can function? Even the most fluent speakers can struggle to explain this stuff, so watch their behaviour for clues and ask questions.

Once you have identified the things that they love, you can look through those to see what will have the most beneficial effect on their future. Can you teach turn-taking through using Lego Therapy, for example? Can you encourage their computer skills by getting them to develop a presentation on their interest?

What if the special interest isn't age-appropriate?

It is hard to see your child (who adores Barbie), watch her peers and friends at school move on to following pop groups, or developing other interests and stop playing with the things that they used to enjoy together when her interests haven't changed. This can be a source of great unhappiness, especially for girls who tend to be more socially motivated and may really want to be able to spend time together. As with any special interest, if it causes no harm, then just relax and certainly don't try to remove it.

There are plenty of adults with a love of My Little Pony, Transformers, or Star Wars collectibles for example. What you will probably want to do alongside that is to try to develop an interest that can be shared in social groups. Some of the best secondary schools are fantastic at having a range of lunchtime and after school clubs, which may well appeal to your child.

Getting anything else done

OK, so you have identified the special interest, worked out that it is fine for now and you are using it to bring your child new opportunities and joy on a regular basis. So how do you get then to do the things that aren't part of that special interest? As with many things in parenting, consistency and structure can be your friend! I don't know about you, but a number of years ago when my children were much smaller, my house, home and life, were all rather chaotic. We didn't have any set routines and it was impossible to get them out of the house on time for school. Wind forward a few years, and we now have a set of routines that we follow (most of the time) and the stress of doing the basics is so much less than it was. It took us several attempts to get to something that is mainly functional, and there are still plenty of improvements that we can make, but we have all discussed the end result and committed to try to do it that way!

A tip I picked up from a Gina Davies of 'Attention Autism!' was the use of a now/then board. This is simply a small wipe-clean white board. You hold it landscape in your hand and draw a line down the middle. On the left hand side you draw (or write) what you need to do now, and on the Right you put what comes next. By drawing it in front of the child, you are inviting them to share attention with you on what you need them to do. You are telling them what needs to be achieved, using few words or no words at all and you can put it down in front of the child so that they can remember what they need to do after they have forgotten what you have said.

Ideally, if the 'now' activity is difficult or challenging, it is good to follow this up with something that they will love to do, or something that they will find calming. In this way you can step your way through the day, with the adult guiding what must be done and rewarding them for doing something that you needed to complete. The same principle underpins how we 3-film Saturday. Bedroom tidied first/ then 3-film Saturday.

Building long term skills

One of the things that we want most for our children is that they are able to live a life that is fulfilled and happy. What that means in reality will vary hugely from person to person. Some autistic people will need life-long support, but can still experience choices and control in their lives. The biggest single fear of parents of many adults who are cared for at home, is what will happen to their child when they are no longer around. Who will look after them? For others, the worries are more around how they will live in the world, will they be safe, or will some unscrupulous people take advantage of them? Whatever issues your child has and whatever age they are, one of the best ways to deal with this completely reasonable fear is to work out what the situation might be, and to develop a plan of action to address the biggest issues that you can see. The plan you develop will need to change as the individual's needs change, as they learn, develop and grow, however that is manifested in their life.

There are 3 main stages:

- Plot current strengths.

- What key skills/developments/changes do you want/need them to make?

- Mind the gap! Look at the gap between the two and plan how to make that gap smaller.

Having identified where you want to get to and what you need, break down the actions into smaller steps and get creative about ways to solve each of the issues you have raised. The following example based on a young man who is currently 16 and has a diagnosis of high functioning autism. He loves lessons at school and is doing well academically, but struggles with relating to his peers. His organisational skills are particularly poor and he struggles to remember equipment and homework even when he has done it. He is great at ICT, hosts his own games site and wants to write computer games.

Objective: To enable [INSERT YOUNG PERSON'S NAME HERE] to keep up with his work and thrive in College:

Mini Step	Obstacle	Assets
Get him a laptop for college	Need money	Disabled Students' Allowance/ Sponsorship.
Set up study support	Don't know how the system works at college	Internet research/meet the Learning Support team at college.
Find a student mentor	Don't know how mentoring works	Head of 6th Form at school has experience of mentoring for young people with SEN.
Find the right college	Don't know if he will get a place or where he might go	Research colleges to find ones that specialise in his area of interest, then find out what support is available.
Set up an induction process	I don't know the college well enough to know who to approach	Transitions Toolkit from the Autism Education Trust
Build independence in scheduling his work	He might not get it all done	YouTube has films on how to organise and study at college for ideas.

Planning for the future

It can seem almost impossible to know how to engage your young person in planning for their future when they cannot imagine anything beyond the life they are currently living. Just because it is difficult, doesn't mean that you shouldn't do everything in your power to enable a young person to choose what they like, what they dislike and how to live their life in the future. When the Autism Education Trust (AET) carried out research into what outcomes were appropriate for autistic people, there was a lot of consistency between what the adults with autism and children on the spectrum wanted. Adults wanted to live the life that they choose with an appropriate level of support for them. Young people wanted the same things as any child, but are often more dependent on a parent and many wanted to live with a parent forever. Parents wanted to know that their child was provided for when they die.

Try using a person-centred plan. This is now a requirement for education, health and social care staff working with young people who have an Education Health and Care plan under the Children and Families Bill (2014). An example of a person centred plan is available from the AET.[38] Often used with people who have a learning disability and in social care, these plans are a great way of planning and preparing for the future. It is useful to start from a consideration of what is good now, what would you choose to change and what will you do to get there?

---

38 www.autismeducationtrust.org.uk/resources/person-centred-planning-toolkits.aspx

Chapter 4

Neurodiversity – What Type of Difference and When Does It Matter?

What is neurodiversity?

The term neurodiversity was first used in the 1990s to express the view that variation in the way that brains work in autistic people, dyslexia and ADHD is a natural part of human development and not an illness needing treatment and cure. Terms you might hear used include 'neurotypical' or NT as an alternative to people with a brain difference. It suggests that rather than being sufferers or victims of their condition, it is an inherent part of the person that they are. This is the polar opposite of the medical deficit model, still prevalent in the US, which suggests that people with these conditions are less than normal. Whilst I believe it would be wrong to underestimate the very real difficulties faced by people with dyslexia, ADHD and autism, as a parent, I feel that it is the differences between us that make life interesting. We are just wired differently to 'normal' people (whatever that might be!)

People are never a simple proposition, we are a complex and messy combination of the bundle of genes that we were given, what happened to us in our lives from conception onwards and our lives and experiences – all of which combine to make us the people we are. In some ways that old hoary chestnut of the nature/nurture debate is thrown into relief so clearly here. Were we born this way, or did something happen to make us this way? The best research we have so far suggests that there are no easy answers, and that both genetics and environment affect who we are and how we live.

A 2009 study[39] by Edward Griffin and David Pollak separated 27 students (with autism, dyslexia, developmental coordination disorder, ADHD, and stroke), into two categories of self-view: "a 'difference' view – where neurodiversity was seen as a difference incorporating a set of strengths and weaknesses, or a 'medical/deficit' view – where neurodiversity was seen as a disadvantageous medical condition." They found that although all of the students reported uniformly difficult schooling careers involving exclusion, abuse, and bullying, those who viewed themselves from a difference view (41% of the study cohort) "indicated higher academic self-esteem and confidence in their abilities

---

39 Griffin, Edward; Pollak, David (January 2009). "Student experiences of neurodiversity in higher education: Insights from the BRAINHE project." *Dyslexia* **15** (1): 23–41.

and many (73%) expressed considerable career ambitions with positive and clear goals." Many of these students reported gaining this view of themselves through contact with neurodiversity advocates in online support groups.

Difference not deficit

Why does it matter which view we have? Well, it matters because it dramatically affects how you see the young person in your home, what you choose to do and how you choose to bring them up.

Jim Sinclair gave a speech to the 1993 International Conference on Autism in Toronto.[40]

> *"Autism isn't something a person has, or a 'shell' that a person is trapped inside. There's no normal child hidden behind the autism. Autism is a way of being. It is pervasive; it colors every experience, every sensation, perception, thought, emotion, and encounter, every aspect of existence. It is not possible to separate the autism from the person – and if it were possible, the person you'd have left would not be the same person you started with.*

> *"The autism rights movement focuses on the importance of recognising and respecting the rights of people with autism to be as they are, rather than to try to change them into something they are not. This is why many people in the autism rights movement have a problem with organisations promising to deliver or working towards a cure. That would effectively say that the person that they are is so fractured, so flawed, that they shouldn't exist at all. Looking at the very many people I have met, I find it impossible not to join them in being offended by that assumption.*

> *"If you respect a person's innate value whatever they are like, it is hard to see how having a neurodiverse population would be anything other than a good thing, in the same way that a world full of biodiversity with a range of plants, animals and environments makes us less vulnerable to effects of global warming or other catastrophic change. A diverse population brings greater resilience to challenge. This does*

---

40 'Don't Mourn for us' was published in the Autism Network International newsletter, *Our Voice*, Volume 1, Number 3, 1993.

not mean for one minute that we would not choose to minimise any distress, or not to develop skills and abilities that will make it easier for someone to move through the world, but it does mean that we would never want them not to be in it!"

Diagnostic labels and changing trends

No doubt you'll have the same experiences as number of parents, who find people who say, "It wasn't like that when I was young!" The rates of diagnosis of a whole range of conditions seem to have increased. Although reported numbers have gone up, this is partly a reflection of the fact that, as recognition of autism and other neurodevelopmental conditions increases, people are more aware of the condition so they look for it, and when you look you find. Just in case you wondered whether this was actually the case, just think about what happens when you are looking to buy a new car. Let's assume that I want to buy a VW Polo. All of a sudden all I see are Polos everywhere.

In 2014, at the National Autistic Society's professional conference, Professor Roy Grinker[41] showed that there are over 100 autism organisations across the world. He also demonstrated that the number of people with autism (otherwise known as prevalence) is around 2.64% in the general population. Whilst this seems incredibly high, we have to bear in mind that of all of those people who could potentially come for diagnosis only a proportion of those will come for diagnosis. Given how difficult and possibly distressing the diagnostic process can be, particularly for parents, it seems extremely unlikely that anyone would want to go through that process without a very compelling reason. Indeed. Professor Grinker talked in detail about the way that diagnosis and disabilities are continually framed within historical periods and in different cultural contexts. He tracked the way that the same symptoms we now call autism would have been classified as childhood schizophrenia in DSM I in 1952. Autism was first mentioned in DSM II in 1968 and finally to the changes in the way the diagnostic criteria were made in DSM V, which was published in 2014.[42]

41 Roy R Grinker is Professor and Chair of Anthropology at George Washington University. He is the author of *Unstrange Minds: Remapping the World of Autism*.

42 DSMI, DSMII and DSM V are all versions of *Diagnostic and Statistical Manual of Mental Disorders (DSM)* and is used to classify a range of psychological conditions.

So if the titles that we give to conditions change over time, what is the point in having a diagnosis? (Take a look at Chapter 2 for why that might be helpful). And how secure is that diagnosis? Is it real? In order to assess those questions, we first have to look at how a diagnosis is made. There are no blood tests or genetic tests that you can take that will tell you whether you have any the following: autism, asperger syndrome, dyslexia, dyspraxia, developmental coordination difficulty, and many other neurodevelopmental conditions. That being the case, how do diagnostic clinicians decide whether your child has any these issues? There are a number of questionnaires developed by psychologists to assess the way that a young person's mind works which they will use in combination with questionnaires completed by parents and the school in order to assess whether the child has a particular condition. Ultimately it comes down to a matter of professional opinion and how we classify what we see. Wenn Lawson's story shows how diagnoses can change over time, even if the core features of person's presentation have not changed.

Wenn Lawson's story

Dr. Wenn Lawson, (formerly known as Wendy) is a psychologist, qualified counsellor and social worker and has operated his own private practice for many years. Wenn was awarded fourth place as 'Victorian Australian of the year' in 2008.[43] Originally diagnosed as being intellectually disabled, then in his teens as being schizophrenic. 25 Years later in 1994, Wenn was diagnosed as being on the autism spectrum. He was awarded a PhD in 2009 and describes what it is like to be autistic. He says:

> *"I know that I am alive; I breathe, move, talk and function just like any other Human Being. However, I understand (because it has been said to me) that other people perceive me as being different to them. My difference expresses itself in various ways, (egocentricity, eccentricity, and emotional immaturity) but, in particular, in my uneven skill ability. Life seems to me to be like a video that I can watch, but not partake in. I sense that I live my life 'Behind Glass'. However, at times I am completely taken up with an obsession or a perception that*

---

43 Meaning an Australian from Victoria, not someone from the reign of Queen Victoria!

may dominate my existence and make it easy to stay focused. For me, such times mean that I feel 'connected' to life. Life, for me, takes on meaning and purpose."

He describes his journey and getting his PhD on his website.[44]

What are Autism and Asperger Syndrome?

The National Autistic Society[45] defines autism as "…a lifelong developmental disability that affects how a person communicates with, and relates to, other people. It also affects how they make sense of the world around them. Asperger syndrome is a form of autism. People with Asperger syndrome are often of average or above average intelligence. They have fewer problems with speech but may still have difficulties with understanding and processing language."

Autism is a spectrum condition, which means that, while all autistic people share certain difficulties, their condition will affect them in different ways. Some autistic people are able to live relatively independent lives but others may have accompanying learning disabilities and need a lifetime of specialist support. Autistic people may also experience over- or under-sensitivity to sounds, touch, tastes, smells, light or colours.

There is a lot of variation between autistic people. It is often said that if you met one person with autism you've met one person with autism. Autistic people often find the social world very difficult for them to navigate. They have problems making and keeping friends and understanding what other people need, want and value. Normally, when a child develops language they will understand it first and learn to use it second. Autism is the only developmental condition where young people are able to express concepts and use language that they don't understand.

A young person with Asperger syndrome or high functioning autism is very capable of using complicated complex and intricate language. Many will use language in advance of their years and might even sound like a 'little professor'. Most people that we hear from are those

---

44 www.mugsy.org/wendy

45 www.autism.org.uk

with Asperger syndrome, as they are able to put across their views clearly and effectively, with a few honourable exceptions. It is much more difficult to gather the views of a young person who does not use language and is preverbal.

There are a number of conditions that are considered to be part of the autism spectrum. Although they may present very differently, they are all united by the difficulties in social communication, social interaction and social imagination. You might hear any one of a number of different diagnostic labels including high functioning autism (HFA), pervasive developmental disorder – not otherwise specified (PDD-NOS), childhood autism, autistic disorder, atypical autism, semantic-pragmatic disorder and pathological demand avoidance (PDA). The NAS has some very useful information on diagnostic labels[46] or see the glossary of terms and titles after Chapter 10.

Attention deficit hyperactivity disorder (ADHD) and attention deficit disorder (ADD)

NHS direct defines ADHD as a group of behavioural symptoms that include inattentiveness, hyperactivity and impulsiveness. Attention deficit disorder (ADD) is a sub-type of ADHD. Common symptoms of ADHD include:

- a short attention span
- restlessness or constant fidgeting
- being easily distracted.

ADHD can occur in people of any intellectual ability. However, many people with ADHD also have learning difficulties. They may also have additional problems such as sleep disorders. Like autism and Asperger syndrome, there is no biological test that can be completed; it is assessed by how much difficulty your child is having in at least 2 different environments. If they struggled at school, but not at home, then it is situational, not ADHD. So whether your child feels like a jumping bean (ADHD) or a beautiful dreamer (ADD) they have features in common. What is especially common in terms of school for children with ADHD is a lack of ability to organise and plan their

46 http://www.autism.org.uk/about/diagnosis/criteria-changes.aspx

work and the equipment they need to complete it. It is estimated to affect 2-5% of school-aged children and young people in the UK.

There is controversy over the numbers of children diagnosed with ADD and ADHD, especially in the United States where treatment with medication such as Ritalin is particularly common. It is easy to see how being physically active and alert to any threat would be an evolutionary advantage but less useful if you need to sit still and pay attention in a traditional classroom. Some children with ADHD are also prescribed serotonin for sleep disturbances. There is a funny and thought-provoking TED[47] talk by Geoffrey Robinson that is critical of the rates of diagnosis and treatment for ADHD. We also have to ask ourselves whether the lack of freedom and the lack of flexibility teachers are permitted within a closely defined curriculum fosters the ability of our more divergent thinkers to work effectively.

More children are diagnosed the hyperactive version of ADHD than ADD and these are usually boys. Given how difficult diagnosis is, it isn't a surprise that if you have a dreamy and disengaged girl you are far less likely to pursue a diagnosis than if you have a boy who is swinging from the ceiling and bouncing off the chairs. Teachers have less difficulty managing the class with a quiet girl than with a loud and disruptive boy. At home it tends to be a story of lost equipment, multiple PE kits forgotten, homework sheets forgotten, homework not written down or lost altogether even for activities that they like to do. What most children will ADHD need is a system. Unfortunately children with ADHD tend to struggle with consistency and so are even less likely to follow a system than most, unless it can be worked into a habit! If you live in a household like ours where these issues are not confined to the children, it makes providing additional parental support particularly challenging.

Dyslexia, dyspraxia, dyscalculia and other learning difficulties

The NHS defines dyslexia as "a common learning difficulty that mainly affects the way people read and spell words." Dyslexia is a spectrum disorder, with symptoms ranging from mild to severe. People with

---

47 TED is a non-profit devoted to spreading ideas, usually in the form of short, powerful talks (18 minutes or less). www.ted.com

dyslexia have particular difficulty with:

- identifying small units of sound (phonemes) within a word (phonological awareness)
- remembering lists and strings of words (verbal memory)
- naming a series of colours, objects or numbers as fast as possible (rapid serial naming)
- how long it takes to process and recognise familiar verbal information, such as letters and numbers (verbal processing speed).

Dyslexia has no relation to intelligence level. As many as one in 10 students are thought to have dyslexia. It can really affect their learning and how they function as they grow up. Many adults with dyslexia talk passionately about being called stupid and lazy when they were at school, because they found reading and learning difficult. Famous dyslexics include Whoopi Goldberg[48] and Sir Richard Branson[49] and Steven Spielberg,[50] who talk about their dyslexia in YouTube films. Spielberg in particular says how supportive and helpful his parents were in helping with his school work.

There are a number of other specific learning difficulties that are often thought of together. Dyspraxia is a form of developmental coordination disorder (DCD) affecting fine and/or gross motor coordination[51] in children and adults. It may also affect speech. DCD is a lifelong condition that isn't related to intelligence. Children with DCD have been called 'clumsy', but dyspraxia can also affect the child's ability to organize, plan and coordinate their actions. Dysgraphia is a learning disability that affects the physical ability to control a pen and write as well as the ability to process information. It can lead to problems

---

48 If you haven't seen this amazing film about the impact of her testimony, then do! It is available on YouTube www.youtube.com/watch?v=ZWGINKlhst4

49 Richard Branson talks about his dyslexia with Quinn Bradlee at www.youtube.com/watch?v=HpvF5xCQ7s8

50 Steven Spielberg talks about his dyslexia diagnosis for the first time www.youtube.com/watch?v=4N6RKHOHMJQ

51 'Gross motor coordination' refers muscle areas controlling large movements such as walking and throwing, and 'fine motor coordination' is what you need for small, precise movements like typing, writing and threading.

with spelling, poor handwriting and putting thoughts on paper. People with dysgraphia can have trouble organizing letters, numbers and words on a line or page. It can show when someone has trouble processing what the eye sees and making sense of what the ear hears. The Department for Education defines dyscalculia as: 'A condition that affects the ability to acquire arithmetical skills. Learners with dyscalculia may have difficulty understanding simple number concepts, lack an intuitive grasp of numbers, and have problems learning number facts and procedures. Even if they produce a correct answer or use a correct method, they may do so mechanically and without confidence.' Although little is known about dyscalculia it is thought that as many as 50% of people with dyslexia may also have dyscalculia.

Speech language and communication needs (SLCN)

The Communication Trust says that "Poor language is linked to poor behaviour even in very young children. 2 in 3 language delayed 3 year olds have behaviour problems." It is not surprising that if you can't communicate using words, you will use actions instead to get your point across. What do 'speech', 'language' and 'communication' mean? Although you might hear any of these terms used, many speech and language therapists make a clear distinction between the three terms which parents often find helpful.

Speech refers to the ability to create the sounds that make up language ('b', 'w', 'sh' etc.) clearly and accurately. Language is about understanding, using words and putting them together to make meaningful sentences and larger chunks of language. Communication is being able to initiate and interact with other people whether spoken and verbal, or using other communication aids. Young people may be referred to someone like a Speech and Language therapist if they are not speaking in the way that would be expected for their age.

Disability or special needs?

You are considered as disabled under the UK Equality Act 2010[52] if you have a physical or mental impairment that has a 'substantial' and 'long-

---

52 For a definition of disability go to: www.gov.uk/definition-of-disability-under-equality-act-2010

term' negative effect on your ability to do normal daily acts. 'Substantial' is more than minor or trivial – e.g. it takes much longer than it usually would to complete a daily task like getting dressed. 'Long-term' means 12 months or more – e.g. a breathing condition that develops as a result of a lung infection. Several conditions are explicitly named in the guidance on the act. They include developmental conditions, such as autistic spectrum disorders (ASD), dyslexia, dyspraxia and learning difficulties.

The government gives the following examples:[53]

> A six-year-old child has been diagnosed as having autism. He has difficulty communicating through speech and in recognising when someone is happy or sad. Without a parent or carer with him he will often try to run out of the front door and on to the road to look at the wheels of parked or sometimes passing cars, and he has no sense of danger at all. When going somewhere new or taking a different route he can become very anxious. This amounts to a substantial adverse effect on his ability to carry out normal day-to-day activities, even for such a young child.

Examples of children in an educational setting where their impairment has a substantial and long-term adverse effect on ability to carry out normal day-to-day activities:

> A 10-year-old girl has learning difficulties. She has a short attention span and has difficulties remembering facts from one day to the next. She can read only a few familiar words and has some early mathematical skills. To record her work in class she needs to use a tape recorder, pictures and symbols.

> A 14-year-old boy has been diagnosed as having attention deficit hyperactivity disorder (ADHD). He often forgets his books, worksheets or homework. In class he finds it difficult to concentrate and skips from task to task forgetting instructions. He often fidgets and makes inappropriate remarks in class or in the playground.

---

53 See also the guidance on Disability in the Equalities Act at www.gov.uk/government/publications/equality-act-guidance

In both of these examples reading, writing and joining in with activities in class and in the playground, which are all normal day-to-day activities, are badly affected.

The definition of what makes a 'Special Need' is much less clear, and the boundary between special needs and disability is intentionally quite blurred. Many of the conditions mentioned above are counted as a Special Educational Need (SEN) but would not automatically qualify as a disability. There is a general movement away from a hard and fast categorisation of diagnosis as disability. The legislation does include a consideration of how severely the condition affects the person involved.

So what does it all mean? Well, that depends on how badly your young person is affected. If they are able to cope, most of the time, without help, then the impact is going to be minor. If, on the other hand you have a young person whose anxiety level is so high as a result of their autism that they are unable to leave the house without support then they would qualify as a disabled person. There is range of help available through the 'Local Offer'[54] which might apply to your young person. The picture is a very complex one and I would strongly suggest that you get specific advice. In the UK you might like to start with http://www.gov.uk or look up the information provided by your Local Authority.

Mental health. What's the problem and why does it matter?

People with autism or Asperger syndrome are particularly vulnerable to mental health problems such as anxiety and depression, especially in late adolescence and early adult life. Tantam & Prestwood[55] and Ghaziuddin[56] et al found that 65% of their sample of patients with Asperger syndrome presented with symptoms of psychiatric disorder. The problem appears to be even more pronounced in children,

---

54 In the UK, under the 2014 Children and Families Act, Local Authorities have to specify what services are available in their area, the 'Local Offer' which varies from place to place.

55 Tantam, D. and Prestwood, S. (1999). *A Mind of One's Own: a guide to the special difficulties and needs of the more able person with autism or Asperger syndrome*. 3rd ed. London: National Autistic Society.

56 Ghaziuddin, E., Weidmer-Mikhail, E. and Ghaziuddin, N. (1998). 'Comorbidity of Asperger syndrome: a preliminary report' in *Journal of Intellectual Disability Research*, 42(4), pp279-283

according to the National Autistic Society's 'need to know campaign'. They state that "over 70% of children with autism also have a mental health problem [but] children with autism can have good mental health just as anyone else can."

Why is mental health such a problem for young people with special needs? Young people who are having a lovely time at school making friends, interacting freely with a full and varied social life outside school will tend to have fewer mental health problems. However, sadly this is not the case for a large number of the young people that we love. They struggle with relationships, they struggle to express themselves, and they struggle to feel part of the society that could have supported them. They are also particularly bad at asking for help when they need it.

A number of children go on to develop anxiety disorders and depression at an unusually early age as a result of their isolation and their inability to deal with normal life. Anxiety is such a severe problem for people on the autism spectrum that it is often described as an iceberg where what you see above the surface is behaviour as a result of the anxiety that they are operating under on a daily basis. There is often a mismatch between what you might expect a young person to be able to do and what they are able to do. They might be able to do something in one environment, but not in another which can be very frustrating for them. If the young person is aware of the difference between the two, it can be especially hard to cope with. Children with special needs are far more likely to be bullied, which can be especially damaging if they are unable to tell anyone, or are not fully supported.

Single dual and multiple diagnosis – the joys of disability bingo

All of our young people are individuals. The reality of their conditions and how they affect them in daily life is complicated, overlapping and messy. There are common features across a lot of the developmental conditions, which mean that it can be very difficult to differentiate what is autism from what is ADHD from what is dyslexia from what is dyspraxia. Many of those conditions have issues with the part of the brain that organises, plans, initiates and sequences information. They can also impact on impulse control. If you have a young person who is terrified of loud noises, they are far more likely to run into the road. If they don't understand the social rule that you should take it in turns to talk, they are far more likely to interrupt. When you go for a diagnosis, the clinician will look at the biggest issues at that time. Few will look for dual or multiple diagnoses.

It seems to be the case that if you have one area of difficulty you are far more likely to have another to go with it. Professionals will call these 'co-occurring' or 'co-morbid' conditions. So if you have autism you also quite likely to have ADHD, if you have dyslexia you're far more likely to have dyscalculia. The rates of OCD and autism are higher than you would expect. Clinicians looking at diagnosis of girls with autism have suggested that there might be a link between anorexia and autism. This is because many people on the autism spectrum have very particular approaches to food and may well follow a very restrictive diet.

Diagnosis can be difficult. It requires a detailed history and lots of observation, but is very dependent on what a parent says, and how the child behaves in the clinic on the day. Some children are so textbook that it makes it easy, but not all. Given that every child is individual, and how they present varies so dramatically, it can be very difficult to unpick what is actually going on. This is why it takes a skilled clinician and a multidisciplinary team to come to a reliable diagnosis.

Sensory differences – what you perceive is your reality

A number of children have specific issues with sensory integration. This is where the senses don't work together properly with the brain. The majority of people with autism (where they are able to) tell us that they experience their senses very differently to most people. There are seven main sensory areas.

1. Sight
2. Hearing
3. Touch
4. Taste
5. Smell

6. Balance

7. Body Awareness

Autistic people tend to be either highly sensitive or under sensitive to sensory information and will react differently as a result. So for example one young man I know hates the feeling of labels in clothes, but loves soft jersey cloth. Another can't bear the sound of bells and was so anxious at the thought of when the bell was going to ring in school that he couldn't concentrate on the lesson. Other children don't get feedback from their bodies in a normal way. So they might walk on their toes or flap their hands or arms when they get excited. There are people who love to wear tight clothing, or always wear a hoodie so that they can cover their ears. Thy might wear gloves so they can feel where their fingers end. The profile of each and every child is different and they may not be able to tell you anything other than the fact that they are uncomfortable. This is where you get to be a detective. You sit down, and watch what they do, and how they do it. This will give you the clues you need even if they are unable to talk to you.

There are young people who have specific issues around sight and visual integration which can affect whether their brain can make sense of what their eyes are seeing. Some cannot see or recognise faces accurately, and may use other cues such as voices to identify people. One young man I know only sees a swirling mass where other people can see features. As you can imagine, this makes it very difficult for him to be able to respond to non-verbal cues. He just can't see if someone is smiling at him or frowning. Robyn Steward (an adult woman with autism) can't identify faces well, so uses people's footwear and voices to identify them.

The difference between boys and girls

Boys and girls are different. They tend to like different things, and even see the same things in very different ways. What counts as normal is not the same across both genders. So what might worry parents and teachers in a boy might be different to what would worry them in a girl. The diagnostic assessments used for autism for example look for things like lining up trains in a row, or looking at car wheels for their movement rather than playing pretend with them. They underestimate the ability of girls on the autism spectrum to 'act like' their friends whilst being very different. As a result, fewer girls are diagnosed with autism than boys. The 2011 report from Judy Gould and Dr. Jackie Ashton-Smith identified the different ways that girls with autism present.[57] For example:

- Girls are more able to follow social actions by watching other children and copying them, perhaps masking the symptoms of Asperger syndrome (Attwood, 2007).

- Girls are often more social and are involved in social play, but are often led by others and many have one special friend.

- Evidence suggests that girls have better imagination and more pretend play (Knickmeyer et al, 2008). Many have a very rich and elaborate fantasy world with imaginary friends. Girls escape into fiction, and some live in another world with fairies and witches for example.

- The interests of girls in the spectrum (such as animals, horses and classical literature) are very often similar to those of other girls, but it is the quality and intensity of these interests that is different. Many obsessively watch soap operas and have an intense interest in celebrities.

The prevalence of autism in girls has historically been much lower than in boys. A figure of one girl is diagnosed per 4 boys was always quoted. More recent estimates of girls and women referred to the Lorna Wing centre in Bromley suggests a much higher proportion of girls on the spectrum. GPs used to make the assumption that if it was a girl without profound learning difficulties, it was unlikely to be autism. Boys are also more likely to be diagnosed with ADHD, whilst girls with ADHD less likely to be recognised.[58] In ADHD, as in autism, most studies only looked at the condition in boys. Another study found that ten

---

57 Dr Judith Gould and Dr Jacqui Ashton Smith. Missed diagnosis or misdiagnosis? Girls and women on the autism spectrum. Good Autism Practice, May 2011 pp 34-42.

58 www.psychcentral.com/lib/adhd-and-gender/0003126 gives a good summary of recent research.

times as many boys were diagnosed with ADHD as girls[59] – whilst dyslexia is also more common in boys than in girls, and the brains of male and female dyslexics are different too.[60]

Where can I find out more?

When most of us have a problem, we tend to turn to family and friends. Unfortunately, the level of understanding of special needs in the general community tends to be low. Having a child with special needs can be very isolating for parents. You are unlikely to get helpful and informative information from the people around you unless they have specific interest in an area. Talking about issues that your child has is not usually the first thing you will do with a complete stranger. So where else can you go? If you have a concern, one of the first people that you might try is your child's teacher, year manager, or the SENCO (Special Education Needs Coordinator)/Inclusion Manager of the setting. The SENCO is a good starting point. You should also consider consulting your GP. They can refer you to specialist services such as CAMHS (Child and Adolescent Mental Health Services). If you do get a diagnosis of your child, you will normally be offered some additional information. How useful it is varies widely from place to place in terms of depth and quality. It is good practice for parents to be offered an explanation of what the diagnosis is and what it means, and to be signposted to local services and parents' groups that provide help and support for that specific condition.

The other source of most of us search these days is the Internet, but information on the web should come with a health warning. Some information and providers that appear at the top of search terms, especially those who have paid for advertising and so appear first, may not be the most authoritative. Always look for statutory (government-based) sources of information first. Reliable information can be found

---

59 Joseph Biederman, Eric Mick, Stephen V. Faraone, Ellen Braaten, Alysa Doyle, Thomas Spencer, Timothy E. Wilens, Elizabeth Frazier, and Mary Ann Johnson: Influence of Gender on Attention Deficit Hyperactivity Disorder in Children Referred to a Psychiatric Clinic, *American Journal of Psychiatry* 2002 159:1, 36-42.

60 Are More Boys than Girls Dyslexic? Does sex matter when it comes to dyslexia? Post published by J. Richard Gentry Ph.D. on Apr 08, 2014 in *Raising Readers, Writers, and Spellers* (on www.psychologytoday.com/blog/raising-readers-writers-and-spellers).

from health services such as NHS Direct and government funded bodies. Another really good source is disability-specific charities, many of which will provide fact sheets, support parents groups and some even run helplines that can give you information and support. It is fair to note however, that all charities have limited income, so it may be difficult to get through. Many people find that sharing information with parents in the same position as yourself is incredibly helpful. Some charities run local branches so have a look for those. Where national bodies and charities can give you an overall perspective, it is really only parents in the same area as you using the same facilities, the same schools, and the same diagnostic teams who will be aware of the local picture in the same way. Under the Children and Families Act 2014, all local authorities in the UK have a duty from September 2014 to develop a "local offer" of services available. What is included in that will, of course, vary widely.

Chapter 5

Surviving Competitive Parenting – Of Course It's Personal!

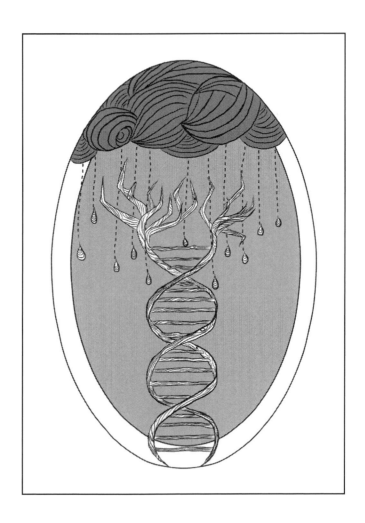

Thunder on the horizon – when someone else spots something you haven't noticed.

So many of us have been there. You're sitting on the floor with a clutch of parents and a bunch of children who are crawling, walking, rolling around, and the mums are all talking. It seems to start okay, at first all you talk about is lack of sleep and irritating family members who seem to have a better idea about how to do everything. But then, you get the first indication that other children are doing things in a different way to yours: "Oh, Johnny has been walking for weeks now!" Maybe you've been going to your parent and toddler groups in a local church hall. It is really loud and your child just sits there with their hands over their ears screaming. Some kindly person sidles up to you, and suggests that your child might like somewhere a little quieter for a few moments. You pick them up, and walk out. The child quietens down, your nerves are in shreds. As you are gathering your thoughts together, the nice middle-aged lady comes out again. She says, "How is he now? My son was just like that at playgroup. Have you ever thought he might be autistic?" Or you're in accident and emergency when the nurse who is examining your child for the after effects of a piece of swallowed Lego comments, "My word! You've got your hands full haven't you?" As your child bounces all over the treatment room.

Given the level of exhaustion that most of us feel most of the time when bringing up small children, your first reaction is likely to be a world-weary sigh. But then, when you have chance to think it through you start to have a nagging feeling that something might not be quite right. If it were just one person, in one place, you would probably write it off as not being important. But when your child's nursery teacher tells you there might be a problem, it's probably time to start paying attention. As a parent of a young child, you are bombarded by information about we what we should do, how we should bring them up and all manner of useful (or otherwise) advice. Some of those sources of information can be really helpful – especially if the child that we talking about is your first. After all your child is doing what your child does, and you have no experience of a range of other children unless you have worked in childcare, teaching or a similar profession.

Why hasn't your child... (insert milestone here) yet?

To know whether there might be a problem, you need to know what normal development looks like. Fortunately there are some amazing resources around that will explain the milestones for normally developing children. NHS Choices Birth-to-Five timeline[61] walks you through what is normal development for children. The Centre for Disease Control in the United States publish a really useful list on the internet which lists the developmental milestones each age of child.[62] Having had two children with special needs, the one thing I wish I had done looking back, is to record when they did things. This information would have been really helpful when looking at assessment later. The only problem that I had with all of these developmental milestones sheets is that there is so much information in them it all looks a bit overwhelming, but bear in mind that what you are looking for is simply to identify where there might be an issue. I have suggested what information would be useful in Chapter 3.

At this stage it is important to realise that everybody develops in their own way. Not all children will develop at the same pace as others. Some have other issues in their lives that will bring about delays in development and it is important not to assume that this will automatically affect them for life. Early development is really important in laying down fundamental skills for life especially in terms of communication. A child who cannot communicate will struggle to learn. What we do know, is that when early interventions are put in place, children have much better outcomes as a result. There is now research that can identify possible autism in babies under the age of one by following where they look. Early intervention is when help is provided as soon as possible after diagnosis, not necessarily early in a child's life.

At this stage there is a huge temptation to start diagnosing your child yourself. Trust me, this is a really bad idea. Firstly, your child may have no problem at all and you could be worrying yourself over nothing. Secondly, the process of diagnosis is a very specialist one and is definitely best arrived at with the help of experienced professionals.

61 www.nhs.uk/Tools/Pages/birthtofive.aspx#close

62 www.cdc.gov/ncbddd/actearly/milestones

Thirdly, your child needs you to be their parent, not their doctor. Your child has a special relationship with you that they almost certainly have with no one else. It's not that you can't find out information, or that you might not be right, it's more that your child needs you to be their mother or father.

From the moment you acknowledge that there is something different about your child, you step blindfolded onto a rollercoaster of emotions, ups and downs, frustrations and joys that you weren't expecting. You have no idea where you're going, you can't tell what can happen next and the destination is unknown. Being so out of control can be really scary! People who like rollercoasters tell me that being out of control is half the fun. The important thing to recognise, is that this feeling of fear, anxiety, uncertainty and dread is absolutely normal. Amazingly enough, other people have taken this ride before and survived or even thrived so you can too. You never know, you might even get to enjoy the view!

Doesn't everyone do that? – We all do in our family!

So many of the conditions that we are talking about in this book run in families. If there is one child with autism in the family for example the chances of any other children having a diagnosis are higher. One of the main things that professionals working on a diagnosis will look for when they talk to you is evidence of similar things in close family members. It makes it particularly difficult when trying to decide whether something is actually an issue that needs diagnosis or just the way things are in your family. Were you late learning to read? Does the child's father, grandfather or uncle hate social occasions? Was your grandmother particularly clumsy?

Families can be fantastic in making homes that really work for their family members. This often happens without even realising it. If you have ever spent time in another person's family, you might be amazed to see how differently the family operates. Some families are really loud and noisy. Others are incredibly quiet. Each and every one has their own set of rules they follow, whether explicitly or not. If you hate social occasions for example, you're unlikely to specialise in big parties. If you struggle with reading, you are far more likely to have practical or physical hobby than sit down with a book. There is something really glorious about a family who enjoy similar things. If that is you, relish it! Whilst others realise that what each individual needs can be very different to the rest of the family. Family activities have to be balanced far more carefully to make sure that no one gets left out when everyone likes different things.

You might worry that your genetic background has caused this problem for your child. Although genetics undoubtedly play a part, they are by no means the whole of the picture. It is also worth thinking about the strengths that your family brings. Functionally, if you are managing most of the time you can't be doing all that badly. In your darker moments, when you look at your child and wonder if they will ever be okay, remember that there is always hope and that your worst fears are just that, fears, and not reality. Don't forget to dream for them too. No-one really knows what the potential for any child is, so don't believe anyone who tells you that they know.

Your child is not "accessing the curriculum"

Of all the phrases that can be used to explain to a parent that there is something potentially wrong with their child, I think this one is my least favourite! At the time I didn't even know what it meant. I now understand that it was an attempt by the nursery to say something to me in a way that was not threatening or upsetting. Unfortunately, I really don't think it worked. All that happened was that my mind went in ever decreasing circles trying to work out what it meant.

Teachers have a very specific set of skills and knowledge that they are trying to pass on, even with very young children. They also have expectations of how a normally developing child would be able to engage with the lesson. When I was told that, I didn't hear anything else. I didn't understand what they were trying to tell me, and I was trying to see what they meant. The best teachers sat down with me and explained in detail what it was that they felt was getting in the way of my child's learning. They also explained what they would expect to see, and what my child was doing and the difference between the two.

In retrospect, maybe we should have acted earlier. I had the upsetting experience of all four nurseries attended by my children telling me that there was an issue with them. At the time, it felt as if the nursery staff were overreacting, especially when the doctors told us not to worry. When the children didn't grow out of it, and didn't develop in the way that was expected, we looked back over their development and realised that there had always been a problem.

"Oh but it's far too early to diagnose them with…"

Knowing everything that I know now about the importance of early intervention, and how much it can help children develop, I can only feel frustrated at the lack of help that we found that at an earlier stage. It felt as if at that time most medical professionals were following the watchful waiting principle. Generally that's quite sound, in that it means that the children are on the books, and that they are being monitored, but no action is currently being taken. In theory that is fine, but if there are increasing problems, you do need someone to keep pushing to get something done, whether this is a parent, or helpful staff at school. So what is the pathway that you should follow? In many cases, the first person to notice will be an education professional. This could be someone at your child's nursery, or at the school. Teachers cannot diagnose, they can only suggest that there might be an issue, but they can also be your ally in getting a diagnosis and appropriate support.

The time at which you might be seeking a diagnosis is highly variable. It will depend on the issues that your child faces, how severely they are affected, and what the condition is. Whilst autism can now be detected much earlier, it is much harder to pick up and diagnose dyslexia before most children would be able to read. This means that it takes longer to get appropriate support. Even children who read really early may well need additional extension and support in schools and many exceptionally bright children also have special needs in another area. This is called dual exceptionality.

In practice you will probably need to visit your GP or medical professional. If the concerns that you have are also echoed by the child's school or nursery, then they are far more likely to agree that a referral for assessment is appropriate. The very nature of general practice means that lots of GPs are not expert in learning difficulties. It will help them no end if you are aware of the developmental milestones that your child should be reaching, and are able to explain to them the ones that they have missed or have not yet achieved. Waiting lists can be very long, so prepare yourself to be in it for the long haul. On the plus side, this gives you time to gather together your evidence and to think of examples that demonstrate the issues that you want to talk about.

Parents under siege in the playground

When your child is behaving in a way that other people don't understand, it can provoke less than positive reactions from other parents. This can be especially difficult when it was a parent with whom you were close in the past but who has now decided that your child is no longer suitable as a playmate for their child. This hurts. Within a matter of weeks, you can go from being someone who always had someone to talk to when you go to pick up your child to someone who is a pariah in the playground. If you are unfortunate, and your child has managed to hit, kick or bite another child, the other parent might tell you off as if you were there telling them to do it. Any sane person with chance to think it through, would know that you hadn't done that. However if someone attacks your child physical or verbally, it is completely normal for a parent to become defensive, angry, and aggressive. As a result you can very quickly find yourself on your own.

So why would someone who was your friend act this way? Usually, it's because they don't understand what has happened. Few parents have any knowledge of special needs, and of the behaviours that children may show as a result of conditions that they have. They fear that their child will pick up the same behaviour. When people don't understand, it is really easy for them to condemn. You'll often hear them say, "I wouldn't let my child do that!"

There are several ways to protect yourself from this sort of situation. I found that turning up at the last possible moment was a great way to avoid standing round on my own for ages. It also helps, if you have other people who are supportive. This could be a member of staff in the school, or one of your friends who doesn't have a child of the same age. Some parents throw themselves into activities. I heard of one mother who started a Master's degree just at the point her child was being diagnosed and she was going through marriage breakdown. Whilst it might seem crazy for her to take on so much, it gave her a different focus and a distraction. It gave her time out, and an environment where she had an identity that wasn't solely tied up with her child. Other people might start a new job, take up a new hobby, refurbish the house, or anything that gives them something different to do. It is really important to change the perspective that you operate from when you feel like you are under siege and are hanging on by your fingernails.

Of course it's personal!

Standing in the playground at school and reacting the way that children react is never a good thing. So why are you getting so riled? When you and your family are under attack because you have a situation that you don't understand it tends to provoke a fight, flight or freeze response. You are simply reacting to a threat. Some people will fight and get aggressive, others will get away as quickly as possible and some will stand like rabbits in the headlights unable to move or act. If you find that your ability to think has been compromised and you feel an overwhelming urge to do something that you know isn't constructive the chances are that it is a response to the amount of stress that you are under.

Sleep is really important for higher functioning brain skills like thought, reason, and the ability to think things through. Unfortunately, this is something that few parents of children with special needs get anything like enough of. Sleep disturbances are very common, in children with ADHD and autism, and in most households when the children don't sleep you don't sleep. There is so much going on in your life, so many additional tasks to manage, so many problems to solve that even if your child is asleep you may well not be. Some children are just incredibly challenging to parent. They might have very high support needs or maybe functioning generally very well but with such poor impulse control that you are always on alert for the next crisis. The net effect of all of this is exhaustion. If you find yourself in this position get professional help to resolve the sleep issue so that you can deal with all the other things more effectively.

There will be periods in your life where the emotions that you are going through will make it very difficult for you to react logically, thoughtfully and helpfully in relation to other people and your child. No matter how calm and constructive you are normally, if you are in a state of emotional turmoil, for whatever reason, you will not be able to access those skills. So what can you do? The first thing is to recognise that it is normal. Periods of stress, unhappiness and turmoil are a part of life and not an indication of failure or weakness. If you're distressed, acknowledge that. If your child came to you sobbing you would look for ways to comfort them. You would think about what helps to calm them and make them feel safe and secure and you would do it. Why should it be any different for you? Why would you deserve less care and consideration than your child does?

Being able to respond is so much easier if you have adequate support around you. This is not a sign of weakness, whether you are male or female. You might have to look quite hard to find it though! Think of the family, friends or colleagues who are in a position to give you help and support, or find a parents' group to join. What that support does is give you time, space, and a different perspective to be able to organise your resources more effectively. Many schools have access to counselling and other support services that are available to families. Feel free to use them.

Dealing with defensiveness

Time and again you may have to be the grown-up, logical, constructive person in the conversation whether you feel like it or not! Whatever the reason is for your meeting with your child's school, getting angry and confrontational will get you nowhere. You will have a number of conversations with people over time that are just plain difficult. In the same way that you don't want to be told that there is something different about your child, the head won't want to be told there is something wrong with their school. Your child is hurting, scared and doesn't want to go to school, and yet you have to send them by law (unless you have agreed with the authorities that they are being educated outside school). But things are happening to them, and you can't protect them, much as you want to. The best way to deal with this difficult situation is to do the following:

1. Understand your emotional state

2. Acknowledge the other person's point of view

3. Focus on a constructive outcome

Whether you're in a meeting, in the playground, or in the supermarket, the same thing applies. Try to see the other person as doing the best they can at the time. It doesn't matter whether you think the person is a complete idiot or not, it is best not to react as if they are!

Preparing for meetings – focus on the positives

Life can be hard. And sometimes we feel like we bounce from one incident to the next. But just occasionally something goes right. A meeting with the SENCO goes well. You find a way of working with someone, or you discover something that will help you with your child. When you spend a lot of time going from problem to problem, it can be very tempting to assume that problems are all that there is. So it can be really helpful to record when things are actually going right for a change! I have a 'glory file' where I keep examples of things that have gone right. Especially when there is a letter from someone else saying how well you've done.

1. **Preparation** – When you are preparing for a meeting, it is really important to think about what you want to get out of it. Identify what would be a good result, what you need to achieve, and how you're going to get it. Start with the end in mind.

2. **Positive expectations** – Having identified what you want, picture in your mind what it will be like when the person agrees with you. If you know them already, imagine how happy they will be to be able to help, feel the relief that will flood through your body when you know that you're solving the problem you went into sort. Be proud of what you've achieved. Feel the spring in your step that happens when you know you've done the best possible thing for your child for this moment.

3. **Look for win-win situations** – Your chances of being successful in negotiating what you need your child are much higher if you are able to look for a situation that benefits both you and the person you're working with. Put yourself into the other person's shoes for a bit, and imagine what it might be like to see your child from their point of view, think about how the solution that you're proposing will be good for them. So for example, if your child is being disruptive in class because they're reacting to being teased by other children, look for a solution that focuses on them being able to stay in the class, actively learning and developing solid relationships with other class members. Then you can discuss how you and the school can work together to achieve that goal.

4. **Offer to help** – You are the expert in your own child and how they think, feel, and act. You have expertise, and offering to help work with the teacher to sort out the issue could be very valuable to them. If there are other resources that you have then please offer, whether it is your time or expertise.

Stop – listen – reflect

There will be times you are told things that you do not want to hear, are surprised by, and may not want to believe. Before you get into a fight with the person who is telling you something you don't want to know, just stop for a second. Ask yourself if this could be true, see if it fits with the information that you have already. Remember that it is entirely possible that your child behaves very differently in a school setting than they do when they're at home, especially if they are a teenager. If it doesn't fit at all with what you know, feel free to share with the person that you're talking to, that you're surprised. You can also tell them why. If you give them an example of how this doesn't match the person that you see, of how their behaviour seems dramatically different, then you are more likely to build credibility with the other person that you're talking to. They may not agree with you, but they will see why you are not automatically agreeing with them either. If in doubt, stop and breathe!

If you're going to resolve the issues effectively, you have to listen actively to whatever information you can get. You might like to start by asking open questions, such as "so tell me what he was like in class today?" Or "what happened just before the incident?" Or "what did you see and why do you think he might have reacted like that?" If nothing else it will give you time to marshal your thoughts, give you a slightly different perspective and help you to understand the point that the other person is making. This is hard to do. You need to come to the situation with a problem-solving mind set. In order to be in a position where you can listen effectively, analyse the problem, and respond calmly with possible solutions, you need to temporarily get as much emotional distance from the fact that this is your child as possible. Try imagining it is someone else's child rather than your own. Do anything you can to take the emotional heat out of this discussion.

Sometimes, no matter how effective you are in a meeting, there is something you forgot to say, or something you think about afterwards, that can really shed light on the issue that you're seeing. Make notes at the time, or ask for a copy of the notes if the other person is doing that, and agree that you might need some time to think through what has been discussed, and email through any other ideas you have questions that have occurred to you afterwards. This is a great way to make sure that you are both working on the same question, and that you agree the actions that you will each take. The only problem with this is that you must follow through on the promises that you make. If you don't do that, you can't expect the other person to either! Finally, don't forget to agree whether you need to follow up, and if you do set a date for the next meeting. Put it in your diary, write it on the kitchen calendar, use your computer or phone reminders, do anything to make sure that you don't forget!

The impact of early intervention

Early intervention means that professionals will provide help as soon as possible to tackle problems that have been identified for children and young people. The UK government[63] suggest that early intervention "targets specific children who have an identified need for additional

---

63 *Early Intervention: Securing good outcomes for all children and young people,* DFES, 2010. http://webarchive.nationalarchives.gov.uk/20110208180934/https://consumption. education.gov.uk/publications/standard/AllPublications/Page1/DCSF-00349-2010

support once their problems have already begun to develop but before they become serious. It aims to stop those problems from becoming entrenched and thus to prevent children and young people from experiencing unnecessarily enduring or serious symptoms. Typically it achieves this by promoting the strengths of children and families and enhancing their 'protective factors', and in some cases by providing them with longer term support."

The ability to communicate with other people is absolutely crucial in terms of child development. Without effective communication skills, children will struggle to make friends, learn and enjoy life. Whilst most children develop these skills naturally, a significant number struggle to do so. Over one million children in the UK have some kind of speech language and communication needs (SLCN). There is a golden period before the age of five, when the impact of interventions can have real benefit on the ability of a child to communicate. Children are hardwired to learn faster in the early years, their brains are more flexible, and they learn new things more quickly. Interventions still work even when delivered later, but they tend to take longer to do so.

So what happens if diagnosis doesn't happen until later? Is it too late for early intervention? A piece of research that followed children over a long time,[64] has found that some indicators of poor outcomes are identified for the first time in children between the ages of 5 and 16. For example a 14 year old who begins to develop mental health problems has as much to gain from early intervention as a 2 year old who starts to display signs of communication difficulties. In both cases it is important for the intervention to start as soon as the problem is identified whenever that identification happened. Research from all over the world suggests that acting quickly prevents problems from escalating and gives children the best possible chance of reaching their potential.

So what outcomes we talking about? There are lots of different ways of assessing children in schools. Many governments look at academic performance; in the UK these are GCSEs at the age of 16, but these

---

64 Feinstein L., 2006, *Predicting adult life outcomes from earlier signals: Modelling pathways through childhood,* London: Centre for Research on the Wider Benefits of Learning, Institute of Education, University of London

can be crude measures of success. A typical indicator would be the number of children achieving five grades A to C at GCSE. This makes no allowance for the child's health, emotional well-being, or life skills. The National Curriculum in the UK set out levels for academic achievement until they were removed by the UK government in 2014.[65] There are also a set of measures of progress (P-levels)[66] for pupils unlikely to achieve national curriculum level 1. Special schools are more likely to assess their pupils against P levels and to collect data on other areas of development as well as academic progression.

Parents' evenings and how to survive them (the good, the bad, and the IEP)

Your experience with parents' evenings will depend dramatically on the quality of school your child attends. The best parents' evenings are when you really get the feeling that your child's teacher knows them, understands them and loves something about what they do. I have been delighted by some of the professionalism, enthusiasm, and passion for teaching that I've seen. A really good parents' evening is one where your child is with you, the teacher welcomes you and your child, then they talk to your child about all the things that they like best about them, tell them what they can do to improve, and explain how they will help them to do that. It is better if your child can be there with you. Policies will vary from school to school, and on the age of the child. It is rare to have your child with you at a primary school parents' evening, but it is very much the norm at secondary school. In most secondary or high schools, teachers will see a huge number of children during the week. As a result, when my child was unable to come with me, I took the folder with all their school information in, and a picture of them on the front with me. This meant that whilst I was waiting in the queue to see the next teacher, the teacher could see the picture of my child and know who they were about to be talking to. It also avoids that nightmare moment where you really aren't sure that the teacher knows your child at all.

---

65 www.gov.uk/government/publications/national-curriculum-and-assessment-information-for-schools

66 www.gov.uk/teacher-assessment-using-p-scales

Not all parents' evenings have been as positive. I did spend years going into a hall to be ticked off a list, sit down and look through my children's books. For some reason, we always seemed to be within easy earshot of at least one parent who had lots of positive things to say to their child about how well they had done in a test and how they should easily get into such and such school. When your child is struggling with serious issues of literacy, trying to get to the bottom of the mismatch between what you see in your child and what they produce on paper can feel a bit much. You have the right to ask your teacher about how your child is doing. Children in this day and age are tested almost to exhaustion, so there is no excuse for staff not having that data and being able to share it with you! Any conversation that starts talking purely about behaviour in a negative sense and doesn't recognise the child's strengths is always going to be difficult. Some evenings, the very best thing you can do is to smile sweetly, get through it, and go home to pour a large glass of wine or a hot bath.

It is a fact of life that with a large number of students, and a limited amount of time, you are likely to be offered timed sessions with your child's teacher or teachers. Whilst the timing is usually enough to get to the bottom of any subject-based queries or to see how well your child is doing in particular subjects, this will almost never be long enough if you have a child with particular issues. Do not feel that this is the only opportunity you have to talk to the school about your child. If the school is aware of the issues that your child has, they should have put in place an individual education plan, or provision map to give your child the support they need. Normally you'll be sent one of these at least once a year, and can ask to see the SENCO or inclusion officer in order to discuss what's in it, and how effectively it is working.

Chapter 6

Stamina - Keeping Going When It Seems Impossible

Reality bites – it can be hard

Much as you love your child, there will be days where you just wish the whole problem (but not the child) would go away. That your family could live in some fairy-tale world with meadows of green grass, bright sunshine and clear skies. But we all know that life isn't like that. There are times of great joy, and times of great sadness. Moments where you can't bear the thought of doing the same thing one more time, and other moments where everything has changed so fast that you're desperate for the stability of doing something familiar.

When it gets really, really tough and you can feel yourself coming to the end of your tether remember that nothing lasts forever. There is real peace in understanding that this too will pass. There have been times in my life when I wondered how I'm going to get through the next 30 minutes let alone the rest of the day. And yet, sometimes even in those moments, there can be moments of good, where something positive can happen. Sometimes it is exactly these events that teach you something you need to know, that might give you an insight you can use, or give you something that can help other people.

I remember very clearly the horror of watching my father die in hospital from cancer. On the day that my mother, my father and I took the decision together that he would have no more treatment and that we were moving into end of life care, I went back to the car park to my car after 11pm to discover my car battery was flat. I called out the recovery service and they told me that it was going to be at least an hour before they could get to me. Visiting hours were long over and the car park was nearly empty. The entrance to the car park had a height restriction and most recovery trucks would not be able to get in so I found the parking attendant in his hut. I must have been clearly distressed because when he discovered I had no money to buy a hot drink to keep me warm whilst I waited, he emptied out his pockets and gave me cash. Then he pointed me towards the maternity hospital where I could find a drinks machine, told me how to get in and offered me a warm place in his hut. It was the worst day of my life but I will never forget his kindness.

Sometimes, the best you can do is to put one foot in front of another, take one day at a time and look for something good however deep it's buried. If you can manage to keep your eyes on the prize, remember what is most important, and hold onto that with all your might then you are moving in the right direction.

Triage – what to deal with first and what next

From time to time problems will land on you thick and fast. There will be so many of them, you may be out of ideas and you just don't know where to start. So how on earth do you know which one to deal with first? There are three questions you need to consider:

1. **Does it really matter?** Sometimes we get so caught up in the job of living, sorting things out, and trying to do our best that we can overanalyse things. I have a particular hatred of themed days and non-uniform days at school. Neither of my children were ever very good at bringing home letters, so I never really knew when these days were going to happen. Several times, we would be walking up to school before I noticed that no one else was in uniform. I had visions of my child in floods of tears feeling really left out as everyone else was wearing the coolest outfits. In the last year of primary school for my youngest he turned round to me and said he wasn't bothered. It turns out the worry was all mine, he didn't care at all!

2. **Is it urgent?** As someone with organisational issues of her own, I tend to prefer to do things straight away before I forget. The do it now principle has saved me from so many problems over the years. Just occasionally though, that adds far more pressure than necessary because it's not urgent. Sometimes it's better to schedule a later time to do it, especially when you are waiting for additional information.

3. **Will it have long-term implications?** If something's happened that is causing your stress level to go through the roof, looking at the problem to see how important it will be in future can be a good way to regain a sense of perspective. It may be a big problem now, but is it likely to be a problem next week, next month, next year or when your child is in their 50s?

D.I.V.O.R.C.E and family breakdown

Bringing up a child with special needs day in, day out is inherently challenging and has a negative effect on family income. It is also something that fathers in particular find very difficult for a host of reasons. The autism education trust (AET) report in 2008[67] showed that:

"The economic impact of autism on families in the UK specifically was also highlighted by Knapp and Jarbrink[68] (2001 and 2007), as was its linkage with the increased rate of family breakdown (and as a result, lone parenting)."

Parents can be asked to collect the children during the school day if they are in distress, or because of an incident. It can happen over and over again. Some parents have reported that they are unable to work or have lost their jobs as a result. Imagine never knowing whether the phone will ring, or when you might be asked to collect your child because of something they have done.

One study found that up to 50% of the mothers of children on the autism spectrum, who were screened, had measurable psychological distress[69] (Bromley et al 2004), and obviously parents may be faced with any other form of disability.

When parents are under stress it emphasises any differences they have in attitude as to how the child or children should be brought up. This adds conflict on top of a difficult situation. It takes a very strong couple to be able to work through these issues again and again and again. Many parents separate and divorce rates are higher in parents of children with autism. Sometimes, though even divorce can have benefits for the family. In an interview for the BBC's *You and Yours*

---

67 Dr Glenys Jones, Annette English, Karen Guldberg, Professor Rita Jordan, Penny Richardson, Dr Mitzi Waltz. Educational provision for children and young people on the autism spectrum living in England: a review of current practice, issues and challenges Autism Centre for Education and Research University of Birmingham. November 2008.

68 Knapp, M. and Jarbrink, K. (2001). The economic consequences of autism in Britain, *Autism*, 5, 1, 7-22.

69 Bromley, J. et al. (2004) Mothers supporting children with autistic spectrum disorders: Social support, mental health status and satisfaction with services, *Autism*, 8, 4, 409-423.

programme,[70] author Nick Hornby and his ex-wife, Virgina Bovell talk about how living separately allows them all to have a break. Parents may also have special needs or disabilities themselves so get a double whammy of having to be an incredibly well-informed and resourceful parent regardless of their own needs.

Parental mental health

If you're travelling on a plane with children taking a flight and there is a problem with cabin pressure, oxygen masks will drop down and the air hostess will tell you as a parent to fit your oxygen mask before theirs. If you fit your child's mask first and then pass out your child will probably not be able to help you. Taking responsibility for your own mental health is really important. There's a saying in the South of the USA that goes "if Momma ain't happy, ain't no one happy!" You set the tone for the children in your household which is a hard, hard job when you are all struggling.

One in four people have mental health issues. Many of those will also be parents. Having a parent with a mental illness is really hard on children, impacts on their learning and can have a lifelong effect on their well-being. Your children depend on you to keep them safe. This is especially so when they are less emotionally mature and have much higher support needs. Some children are especially sensitive to the emotional temperature of the people in the room. Whilst they may be completely unable to express their discomfort in ways that other people understand, that does not for one second mean that they don't feel these emotions. We all find it harder to cope with things we don't understand. If your children are in this position, then you need to find extra support for them outside of the family that will help them to cope.

You are especially important to your children, whether they show that to you or not. The relationship they have with a parent is the deepest and most long-standing relationship the child will have, so you do matter. Your wellbeing is important too!

---

70 http://www.bbc.co.uk/radio4/youandyours/features/autism.shtml

Modelling emotional resilience

Given the ups and downs of life, bringing up our children often feels like riding a rollercoaster. Sometimes thrilling, sometimes terrifying, with no guarantee you're going to get safely to the end. You may not have even been asked if you want to get on. The only consolation is that other people have managed it before you. There is something liberating about relaxing into an experience accepting that it might be scary, and just trusting that you're going to make it through okay.

How can you build up your resilience? How can we make ourselves strong enough to ride the waves of adversity rather than being pulled under? How is it that some people can cope with huge amounts of stress whilst others fall apart? Brad Waters identifies the 10 traits of emotionally resilient people.[71]

1. **They know their boundaries** – understanding this difference between who they are at their core and what is causing them temporary suffering.

2. **They keep good company** – resilient people tend to seek out other supportive people who know how to listen and encourage without trying to solve all of our problems with their advice.

3. **They cultivate self-awareness** – when we know what we need and when we need extra help we are more able to ask for it.

4. **They practice acceptance** – pain is painful, stress is stressful, and healing takes time. Stress and pain are a part of life and is better to come to terms with it than to ignore it, repress it, or deny it.

5. **They are willing to sit in silence** – not easy to do, but one of the purest and most ancient forms of healing and resilience building

6. **They don't have to have all the answers** – trying too hard to find answers to difficult questions can block them from arising naturally in their own due time

---

71   Brad Waters. 10 traits of emotionally resilient people in Design your path. *Psychology Today.* May 21, 2013

7. **They have a menu of self-care habits** – this is a list of helpful things you can do that support you when you need it most,

8. **They enlist their team** – resilient people know who is good at listening and who isn't and who will reflect back what we need to hear

9. **They consider the possibilities** – training ourselves to ask what in our current story is permanent and what could change. Our interpretations of stories changes as we grow and mature and gives us the hope that tomorrow things can feel better.

10. **They get it out of their head** – when our thoughts swirling and disconnected we can find relief by writing our thoughts onto paper, exercising or distracting ourselves.

Exercise and stress relief – free endorphins, anyone?

Sometimes what you need most is a change of scene. When you feel like that, just get out of the house, if you can. If there is a responsible adult with whom you can leave your child whilst you walk around the block to think things through, then that is great. Feel free to ask them, go ahead and do it. You might be the sole carer, or maybe there isn't anyone suitable to leave your child with whilst you de-stress, especially if it is late at night. Not everyone has a responsible adult on tap. In which case, you will have to think a little more creatively about ways to get a little space and time for yourself.

Exercise is a great way of making yourself fitter, healthier, and more able to deal with the stresses in your life. Gone are the days where you have to go to the gym for two hours in order to get the benefits of exercise. Recent research has highlighted the value of high intensity circuit training (HICT). High intensity circuit training is where you alternate different exercises for very short periods. Even doing as little as seven minutes a day can improve your level of general health, and reduce the likelihood of you developing type II diabetes. These exercises can be done at home. I bought an app for my iPhone which means that for around the price of a cup of coffee I can follow an exercise regime at home, at a time to suit me. If apps aren't your thing, then there are lots of different ways of exercising without going out or spending crazy money. Many people like using exercise videos. You might think that doing exercise isn't you, but if you do regular exercise, it floods your body with naturally produced 'happy hormones' called endorphins. Regular exercise is proven to reduce stress, ward off anxiety and feelings of depression, boost self-esteem and improve sleep. All things that most of us are desperately in need of.

It's not just a matter of not being sick, we need to aim to be well, fit and healthy. It doesn't feel too much of a stretch to compare parenting to running a set of ultra-marathons[72] back-to-back for years. You wouldn't expect a marathon runner to do that without training, so why would you expect to be able to deal with the challenges you face without preparing yourself physically for the challenge?

I need someone to listen to me!

It is very easy to feel isolated, if there isn't anyone you can talk to. Most of us will have people who can listen but the quality of the listening is also important. The best supporters that we have are those who listen actively to what we say, rather than being those who give us the feeling that there just waiting for us to pause before they talk. You really want someone who listens to the emotions behind what you are saying as well as the words that you say. Your conversation should have a sense of to and fro, reciprocal turn taking and that the person is really paying attention to you (no playing with mobile phones here!)

Many of us, especially women, are particularly fortunate in having at least one supportive friend. They are someone who listens to what you say, understands what you mean, and helps you work through what you need. This doesn't always mean that they will agree with everything you say. Clearly, if all they do is argue with you that wouldn't be any good either. One of the jobs of a really good supporter is that they will show that they understand how you feel, but that they will also be able to disagree, or ask you questions that challenge you without it threatening your relationship.

If you don't have anyone in your personal life who can do this for

---

72 Any sporting event involving running and walking longer than the traditional marathon length of 42.195 kilometres (26.219 miles).

you, there are a number of professionals who might be able to help. It is always better to find someone who has knowledge of the situation you're in. This might be a parent support group who have access to counselling services, or you might want to seek out specialist coaching and mentoring services. There are specialist ADHD or ADD coaches for example (you can find lots of them on the internet by typing ADHD Coach), who can be paid to come to your home and work through the organisational systems that you use. The top five benefits of using an ADHD coach are that they can help you to:

1.   Pay attention to goals long enough to complete them.

2.   Learn ways to self-motivate and stay on task.

3.   Develop structures in your life based on your strengths to help you stay on track.

4.   Develop rituals and routines that you will use and stick with.

5.   Use feedback more effectively.

You do need to bear in mind that there are no formal qualifications for this type of coaching, so look for one who has personal experience and vet them carefully.

How to listen to your child – even if they aren't talking

In the maelstrom of everyday life it is really easy not to listen to each other – especially when there is a teenager in the house. The first thing to do is to stop talking. There are times when you have to say things to your children, but when you are trying to learn about what is important to them is not the time to be taking up the airwaves. You just cannot hear anyone else when you are talking. It is often said that we were given two ears and one mouth, so you should spend twice as much time listening as you do talking. Even if they were interested (and many just aren't) lots of children have a particular problem in processing long streams of audio instructions. If your child can only take one instruction at a time, there is no earthly point in talking at them beyond the first sentence. After that, everything just becomes a long stream of "blah, blah, blah, blah, blah…"

When you are your child's advocate, champion, and parent you have to know what is important to them. You need to know what is bringing them joy, and what is causing them pain and with some children that is really hard to establish. Some autistic people are unable to identify where the pain is happening. All they can do is show through their behaviour that they are in pain. Virginia Bovell, mother to Danny and one of the founders of Treehouse School in London has described how his behaviour is very different when he's suffering from extreme gastrointestinal pain. Some children do not talk, so we have to find other ways of communicating with them, whether that is using an alternative augmentative communication system (AAC), such as symbols, or visual communication systems such as PECS (picture exchange communication system). There is more detail in Chapter One on communicating with children who find talking difficult.

Even with children who are able to talk fluently, the ability to communicate decreases when under stress. Remember back to a time when you were really upset and think about how well you communicated under those circumstances. Your children don't have your level of resourcefulness and experience to call upon. Sometimes all you can do is to watch what they do. Look very carefully at their posture, the way they react if you walk into the room, if they seem more tired or more nervy than normal. They may use gesture or expression. You are looking for changes in comparison to how they normally move, talk and act.

Becoming an expert detective

When you have a child who cannot communicate effectively on their own it falls to you and the professionals who support your child to unlock their world and to enable them to communicate in ours. How well you do this affects how well your child can function, what they're able to achieve and whether they are likely to reach their potential. Knowing the person really well is essential. You have a choice to be the Inspector Lestrade, or the Sherlock Holmes in your child's world. It is impossible to sustain the level of observation every minute of every day, but you can learn to understand the language that your child uses whether physical, verbal or visual. Once you understand how the child communicates, you can use that to give them choice in their own lives.

It can be very difficult to work with child who has communication issues, but it is really powerful to be alongside a child who is struggling and to be able to show them that you understand. They need to know that that they are worth listening to, and that what they think matters. In my mind, there are few expressions of love purer than to express the thoughts in someone else's heart when they are unable to speak.

Problem-solving skills – testing, testing 1-2-3

The problems that you will face as a parent vary hugely from child to child and from moment to moment. Your ability to come up with new and effective solutions will be tested continually, so it is really handy to have some pretty solid problem-solving skills. There are a host of different techniques you can use. Lots of them are available on the Internet free of charge. There are a number of key stages to problem solving:

1. Find out what the problem is.

2. Identify possible solutions.

3. Choose the best solution.

4. Did it work? If not try a different one.

5. Repeat as necessary.

Many people enjoy mind mapping[73] which is especially good for visual learners to help come up with alternative solutions. One of the best ways to identify the problem is to use the six questions: who, what, where, why, how and when. The detail that you come up with here can help you identify possible solutions as well.

It is pretty much certain that your ability to find the right solutions depends on how much you know, your resourcefulness in finding solutions and your ability to implement them. If in doubt, do some research, ask around, and experiment with different options. It doesn't matter how good your solution is if the person who needs to use it

---

73 Tony Buzan *How to Mind Map: The Ultimate Thinking Tool That Will Change Your Life.* Thorsons, 2002.

doesn't like what you come up with. So for example, if you want to develop a system so that your child doesn't forget to take their homework into school, you need to work with them to find out what will help them remember it. Although even your best idea might not work if they have to follow a different process at school, so ask your child's teacher or SENCO what will work from their point of view too.

Learning from the best and finding a champion

There are some problems you just can't solve on your own. The only thing you can do is to change your own behaviour (and even that isn't easy). Assuming that you are really good at problem solving, you might still find that given the ongoing challenge you just run out of ideas. Given how tired you are likely to be, it's entirely possible that someone else with a fresh pair of eyes and a different appreciation of your child might well come up with a really good solution.

If you were to set off to climb the Matterhorn you wouldn't ask someone who had never climbed a mountain for help. You would go to the best, most knowledgeable guide you can find. You might take climbing lessons, join a local climbing club, and watch videos on climbing. You might go to the gym, to build up your muscle, so you're strong enough to do the climb. You'd go to a specialist climbing shop to buy all the gear that you needed the trip and you would find a guide who knows the mountain and can show you the best route to the top.

Your first port of call as a parent is likely to be using local professionals, such as your GP, health practitioners, school staff, health visitors, and local parenting groups. Each of those groups will hold a part of the solution to most of the problems that you will face. If you exhaust their resourcefulness, the next place to look is the national resources, charities, websites, government guidance etc.

Great friends, great support

There are some things that your friends can give you which will make your life more pleasant, more interesting, and more fun! Friends can give you their time, whether that is offering baby-sitting services, because they are the only other person who understands your child, or whether it is just time for you to let off steam by having a bit of a moan. Just make sure that you share your triumphs as well as your pain.

If you have a wider group of friends, they might have either professional or personal expertise which could be really helpful. Maybe you know an occupational therapist? A health visitor or a professional coach who is happy to give you their time and skills free of charge or for 'mates rates'.[74] Many people find great support and comfort from sharing their experiences with other parents who have children with the same condition. Some groups arrange holiday clubs, trips and outings which can help you to feel less isolated.

The most valuable thing a good friend can give you is the really useful mix of support and challenge. There is a real art to knowing when somebody just needs to be told that everything is going to be okay, and when they are making assumptions that need to be challenged to make sure that they have thought all the issues through.

---

74 You get things cheaper if you are a friend!

Chapter 7

Family Dynamics, Siblings and Wider Family

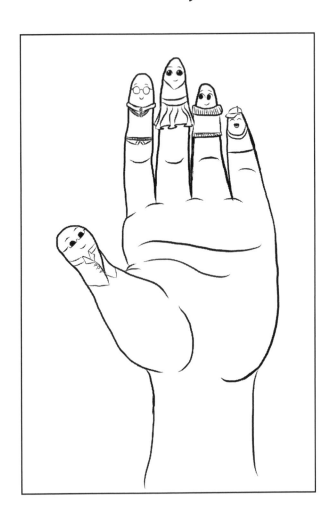

Some things run in families – and some don't!

From time to time when we look at our children, we wonder how much of what they do they got from us, and how much is just because that's who they are. As they grow older, this is usually easier to work out. A long-standing debate in science is whether it is nature (the genetic makeup, character, and inclination of a person) or nurture (the way that they are brought up and their environment), that has the biggest impact on a person. My view is that both matter. Think of someone you know and love really well. Now ask yourself what they are like, and think about why they are like that. Is it their character, or how they were brought up? If I were to use myself as an example, part of what has made me the person that I am today is nature. I'm female, I'm a certain height I have brown eyes and a susceptibility to ear infections. Another part of who I am is related to how I was brought up. I'm an only child, so I spent a lot of time with adults rather than other children, being part of their conversations, so I tended to speak more formally.

We each have a unique genetic imprint, which affects not only our bodies, but also how we see, make sense of and understand the environment around us. It affects the way that our brain is wired, and as a result what we see, feel and experience our world. In a recent TED talk, Wendy Chung[75] describes how genetics plays a much stronger role in autism than it does in diabetes, heart disease or cancer. She explains that in some people, a single gene causes autism, but in others it might be a number of smaller genetic changes. Currently, between 200 and 400 genes are thought to play a part in autism, and how they combine to make the set of characteristics that we see as autism.

There are some things that we know affect the chances of being on the autism spectrum. They are:

1. Older fathers at the time of conception.

2. Events that occur when the foetus is in the mother's womb, including some infections while the baby's brain is developing.

3. Genetic causes.

---

75 Wendy Chung, Autism – what we know (and what we don't know yet) TED 2014

We know that genetics does play a part, but is not a complete explanation for autism, because an identical twin of a sibling with autism only has a 77% chance of having autism themselves.[76] If autism were completely inherited, that figure should be 100% and it isn't. Even two people with the exact same genetic makeup will not necessarily both have autism. Non identical twins who share the same womb, but different genes, have a 31% chance of autism. Brothers and sisters who weren't in the womb at the same time have only a 20% chance of developing autism. The fact that there is a difference between the rates between non-identical twins and ordinary siblings suggests that there may be something happening in the womb which makes autism more likely.

Families with more than one neurodiverse[77] child have a great opportunity to make their home a supportive, functional environment. Providing helpful and supportive strategies for everyone can be the way that your family works, because "that's just the way we do things." You have a free hand to run your home in the way that meets the needs of your family best and it doesn't have to be the same as anyone else. Jennifer O'Toole, an adult with Asperger syndrome and mother to children with Asperger syndrome has written extensively about the fun and laughter of being on the spectrum and has published a book on how to arrange the home so that it supports learning and independence.[78]

Many adults with autism first seek diagnosis for themselves as a result of diagnosis for their child. Damien Milton, an adult with autism, describes how this worked for him. "I only got my autism diagnosis because of my son. When he was 18 months old his mum was concerned he wasn't responding to her. At first my reaction was, 'There's nothing to worry about, he's just like me!' He was diagnosed with autism aged two and it was while I was reading autobiographical accounts of people with Asperger's that I thought, 'I did that as a kid.'"[77]

---

76 Wendy Chung, Autism – what we know (and what we don't know yet) TED 2014

77 Neurodiverse is a non-judgemental term used to describe anyone with autism, ADHD, dyslexia or anyone with a condition that is based on a variety in how their brain works.

78 Jennifer Cook O'Toole, *The Asperkid's Launch Pad: Home Design to Empower Everyday Superheroes*, London: Jessica Kingsley, 2013.

Meeting unequal demands – everyone wants a piece of me!

It's 4 o'clock in the afternoon. You just got back from picking up children from school. Your work phone goes off. One child is screaming and another is talking loudly at you rather than to you about their special interest. You ignore your work phone, bribe the chatty one with chocolate to go and sit in another room, and deal with the screaming child. Your mobile rings, it's the school and there's been an incident today that they need to talk to you about. By the time you finish talking to them, it's time to get tea ready, you have no idea what to cook and you still haven't started sorting homework. At this point, it is worth remembering that not is not just children that suffer from sensory overload! Unfortunately, no one is going to appear at your side, wave a magic wand and create a wonderful nutritious meal for you. Sometimes the kindest, most loving thing you can do for yourself is to plan ahead. There are lots of really useful meal planning sites which can prevent you getting into that nightmare scenario where it's 5 o'clock, you haven't got a clue what to cook and you have no food in the house. When you know you're going to be up against it for a while, you might like to prepare a set of meal kits in advance and freeze them. That way, you can make sure they meet any dietary needs your family has. All you have to do then is get them out of the freezer the night before, make sure they are defrosted appropriately, and then cook them when you're ready. This is one stress you can remove easily, so do!

When you have a child whose needs are greater than the rest the family it will skew the amount of time that you have to spend towards them, and you may well feel guilty about that. No, it's not fair, but it is the reality. In my experience, these things don't stay the same all the time either. You do have to be careful that you don't get into the habit of assuming that because one child has higher support needs at one point in time, that your other child doesn't need you as much. With two very emotionally sensitive children in the house, they usually take it in turns to have a problem and to be the 'easy' one. Imagine my horror, exhaustion, and stress when I discovered that this isn't always the case. And sometimes everybody is having a rough time at once. In which case, you can't ignore anyone, and you just have to take it in turns to work with each of them. It is really important to avoid seeing your child with special needs as someone who always needs to be 'fixed'. They are fine just as they are, but sometimes a situation needs sorting out.

So the first question is what is fair? Fair isn't about giving the same amount of time to each child. It is far more about making sure that each child has what they need in terms of love and attention. We need to show that we can listen to how our children are feeling, not just what they say, and need to find enough common ground to understand them. We have a limited number of hours in the day and can choose how we spend them. We might need to work, to provide food and accommodation for our families and a life for ourselves, but there is time when we are not working and we can choose how to spend it.

So what will work for you? The cartoon family, The Simpsons, always eat together, they talk to each other and spend time together as a family. In a busy family, meal times can be a real opportunity to catch up with each other. We have enjoyed watching particular TV series together, listening to audio tapes in the car and sharing music (of all sorts from classical to heavy metal, to indie pop, to comic songs to gaming theme tunes!). At one stage, we were having a particularly rough time with issues around school. Luckily, it happened in the run-up to a school holiday. It took us going away for me to realise that we as a family are okay, and that the stress and anxiety we were feeling was to do with the situation and was not about us. This revelation helped me to come back with a far more positive and constructive attitude as a result.

Keeping relationships going

When your day-to-day life is so completely absorbed by managing the needs of your children, running the household, and earning a daily crust, it is really hard to keep a good relationship alive with your partner, family or friends. Often though, it is the smallest things that make the biggest difference. Cultivating an attitude of gratitude can be really helpful. It may be is that someone brings you a cup of tea in the morning, or does some other small act of kindness that brightens your day.

Relationships are difficult to maintain at the best of times, let alone when under the stress of raising a child with issues. It is safe to assume that if you manage to raise your child from birth to the age of 18, life will happen whilst you're busy doing it. You don't get a get out of jail free card, just because you already have a lot to cope with. Other people have things that cause stress in their lives too, so they may not always react as positively as you hope. Try not to assume that it's automatically about you if something goes wrong.

Whoever you want to maintain a relationship with, try to find common ground with them. List the things you share, remember what you enjoy doing to do together (or alongside each other), and things that make you feel good. We all need emotional support from time to time, and it is really handy to have people around who are willing, and able to do it. If you're fortunate enough to have people like this in your life, then you must be appreciative to them and thankful that they are in your life. Buy them a little present for no particular reason if you can, send them a card, or just treat them to a cup of coffee. Saying thank you can be a wonderful thing. It makes you feel good, and it encourages them to be supportive again in the future.

Sibling issues

At secondary school most children will do just about anything to be seen as normal. So it can be really tough having a brother or sister who is not seen as being 'normal'. Very few young people in their teens who want to be approached by complete strangers in the corridor school and asked whether they are X's brother/sister. If someone came up to you and said, "Why is your sister/brother so weird?" then you probably wouldn't feel great. Boys and girls are likely to feel upset and most boys are more likely to show that by becoming aggressive which never goes down well at school.

Everyone needs to be recognised as an individual in their own right. This is probably even more important if you have a sibling who is very identifiable, in the street, and at school whether positively or negatively. We all need to be known and loved for who we are, not as some bolt on part of somebody else. So find out what is important to each and every one of your children (if you have more than one of course), what makes them tick and what they love to do. Spend time recognising their successes and supporting their dreams.

It's really easy for resentment to build up if one child feels that the other is getting all the love, care, attention, money and time in the family. But when a child understands why their brother or sister is different and that they aren't doing it on purpose many siblings will go out of their way to love and care for their brother or sister. Without intentionally planning it, I have found myself several times realising that the first child raises the second. Any pretensions you might have had to being a parent to both of your children equally are squashed when you realise how this works. I sat out of sight whilst my eight year old explained to the youngest about how sex and reproduction worked (and did a really good job of it too). Although I did talk to them about sex and relationships several times as they moved through developmental stages, I was deeply impressed at the time.

Mothers, fathers, roles and recognising strengths ...

Men often have a hard time with any form of disability. The biological role of the man in most societies is to provide fit, healthy heirs. So finding out that something might be different about their child is a hugely difficult blow to come to terms with. Men are also often side-lined in terms of the family. This can start as early as in pregnancy, when all of the focus is naturally on the pregnant woman, but it can leave the man without a role to play and fail to recognise the love that many men feel for their baby. Where they have been a couple before and much of his partner's attention was on him, it now gravitates towards the baby. This is an opportunity for the whole family to spend time together, but many men either choose to, or are forced to return to work really quickly when the whole family is making a major adjustment to how it works. It is a chance for a man to grow into becoming a father and feel a depth of love that they would not have thought possible.

Unless the man is the main carer, he is likely to be less involved in the day-to-day reality of bringing up a child, so tend to be less sensitive to signs that something might be different. As a result, men are more likely to think that the mother is overreacting. When a child is showing signs of behaviour which the father also did when he was younger he might feel that the mother is implicitly criticising him, by saying that the child is not ok. She will be worried, and failing to get a supportive reception can drive a wedge between parents.

Fathers can also be excluded by the professionals who work with children. So many reports are of full of 'Mum said' and 'reported by Mum' and may even refer to the fact that the father was not present at the meeting, but they rarely ask why that is the case. Some fathers are fully involved and engaged, but just might not be able to be there on the day. Other fathers are lone parents with full responsibility for the child and will be there at every meeting whilst some men can't cope and run for the hills emotionally or physically.

When partners don't agree

There may be times where you just can't talk about a situation. It's too difficult, you feel too emotional and you just can't think straight. Just remember that that doesn't mean that it will always be like that, or that there isn't way through, it just might take time, space and opportunity for you to be able to talk. The main thing to remember is that you're both trying to do what is best for your child, even if you can't agree what that might be right now. Although women tend to be more emotional, presenting arguments that centre on feelings rather than facts, that by no means suggests that men don't have deep emotional gut reactions to any issue relating to their child.

If you're not sure how best to proceed, think about what you know about your partner and what you want to come out of the discussion. If they like a logical argument, gather your facts together first, think through what you might like to say and how you would like to present it. If you don't know where you stand yet on a decision, there's nothing wrong with having a discussion about what the issues might be. I would suggest however that if it is going to be just a discussion you frame it that way, so that neither of you feels that you're being bounced into a decision before you're ready and have thought through all the things that it might include. Those of us who like things to be visual might like to draw out the discussion listing pros and cons on a large piece of paper to help you to think through what the issues are. You can set a different time to make the decision after you've had time to consider it carefully.

You won't always agree on everything no matter how close you are as a couple, or how much you agree on most things. You don't have to win every argument. Some really aren't worth winning at all. Pick the ones that are most important and if you really believe in your heart of hearts that the issue that you're discussing is vital then go for it. Think through your points, gather supporting evidence and present your case. Even if you have a really strong point, present all the opposing views, and answer them, explaining why they are less important. Don't forget to acknowledge the feelings that you and your partner have, always bearing in mind the aim which is the best possible outcome of your child.

The gift of grandparents

If you're fortunate and have a set of parents whom you love and trust with your children and who happen to live close enough to be convenient then you are really lucky. Grandparents can be a wonderful thing for a child; they are far enough away from parenting to be able to have the perspective that you lack. Grandparents can have an incredibly close bond with their grandchild and can be a friend and confidant in ways that would never be possible with a parent. As someone who was granny-reared until the age of 5 and then every school holiday, I can tell you how strong that bond can be. You won't always agree with them either, but there are few other people on God's earth who will love your child as much as they do.

Sharing the news on your child's diagnosis with a grandparent can be really difficult though. In the same way that sometimes fathers struggle to come to terms with the diagnosis, grandparents are one stage more removed. In their day many conditions didn't have a name. Children were called 'lazy', 'disobedient' or 'retarded'. It might help you to know how long these diagnoses have been around.

- Autism was first described as a condition by Leo Kanner in 1943, and Asperger syndrome first recognised by Austrian paediatrician Hans Asperger in 1944. Both conditions were identified in 1979 as part of the autism spectrum when Lorna Wing and Judy Gould coined the term to recognise the same underlying factors (known as the 'triad of impairments') that apply to a number of conditions which can look quite different.

· • ADHD – Sir George Still (1902) was the first to describe ADHD whilst Franklin Ebaugh (1923) had evidence that ADHD could arise from brain injury

• Although the condition was identified by Oswald Berkhan in 1881, the term 'dyslexia' wasn't used until 1887 when it was created by Rudolf Berlin, an ophthalmologist practising in Stuttgart, Germany.

Given how recent many of these conditions are in terms of diagnosis and understanding, is not surprising if older members of our society struggle to get to grips with what they are. It's very common for a grandparent to say, "Oh, they'll grow out of it." Much of the time, this comes from a place of trying to cheer you up, rather than dismissing your concerns, but if you are feeling sensitive at the time you probably won't hear that. You might like to mention the top 3 reasons which you feel help you to know that the diagnosis is correct and share them. Remember the shock you felt and how little you knew about it, well they are where you were not that long ago. Give them some basic information to help them understand, and refer them to disability specific awareness training if you have any in your area. Many organisations will train any family members including grandparents.

Once your family member knows and understands what the condition is they can begin their own journey of finding out more and learning from your child, who after all is the best teacher. When they're fully informed, a sympathetic grandparent can be a useful sounding board and an ally for you, whether this is just a chat over a cup of tea or coffee, or to come with you for meetings with the school or health professionals for support.

Redressing the time balance – if only time travel were possible!

Okay, so we all accept that perfection isn't possible. In the words of Salvador Dali, "Perfection is nothing we need to worry about because will never get there." But we still want to make the best job of being a parent that we can. So how can you go about working out how you spend your time and helping it to be more balanced? A really good way of understanding the dynamics of how time works in your family is to complete a diary for week. There are three stages to bringing about a change that you like to see. The first is understanding what's happening now, the second is working out what you would like to see, and the third is working out how you get from where you are to where you want to be.

To help plan your family life better, ask yourself the following questions:

- How does your life look now?
- What you do, when, and for whom?
- How much time do you spend at work?
- Who gets most of your attention?
- Is anyone being missed out altogether?
- Is there time for your relationships with other people?
- Do you keep some time just for you, even if it's only 15 minutes?
- Where's the fun?

How would you like your family to work in the future (realistically?)

- What is missing altogether?
- What are you doing too much of?
- What would you like to do more of?
- Who would you like to spend more time with?

What resources do you have that you can use to move it in the right direction?

- Family
- friends
- educational support
- support groups
- statutory support

- knowledge and research.

Now, pick one change, the smallest you can find, and make it. Well done! You've just taken your first step towards making a positive change! Now pick a bigger one and try that. Does it work the way you wanted? If it does fantastic! If not, think about whether there's a tweak that you can make to make it work. Take one step at a time, however small, and remember you are moving in the right direction. Get everyone else to help as much as they can. After all it's in everyone's interest to have a happy family. If the first change worked well, now pick the next and do the same again.

Communication, communication, communication.

Being able to communicate with each other is the most important thing that you can do for the family. We need to connect with each other at some level. For some people this might be the right type of touch (or understanding that touch is painful). For others it's the gift of a loved book, beautifully cooked meal, or the chance to go out and spend time together. Whether the relationship is with your partner, your children, your wider family, or your friends, keeping those lines open is vitally important not only for them, but also for you. What works will depend hugely on who we talking about. So if the only way you can talk to your son is by playing a computer game with them then go ahead and play. If your daughter loves clothes and wants you to buy them a new outfit, assuming you have money, go ahead and do it. If money's an issue, ask for vouchers at Christmas and birthdays so you can still share that experience together.

From time to time, despite your best efforts, things don't go according to plan and your attempts to communicate will fail. When this happens take a deep breath. See if you can work out what went wrong and try something different. Whatever you do, DON'T GIVE UP!

When you're overwhelmed and all you want to do is grab the duvet and pull it up over your head, it's really hard to put yourself out there again and again and again. But one of the most important things in terms of your mental health is making sure that you use the support that is available to you. If you don't see anyone it's hard for people to know that you need help. So get out there and ask. Use the times when this really worked to remind you of how good it is! And do the same to your family reminding them, and reinforcing when it goes well. You will need to do this often, sometimes daily. Praise whenever something works.

Everyone gets special time

There are lots of things in life that we have to do, even if we don't want to. We all need time to do the things that we love, whether we're children or grown-ups. Your child will need time to develop the things that make them feel safe, secure and develop them as a person. Sometimes you can join them in that and sometimes they will just want to be left alone to get on with it, but don't assume that you know which they prefer unless you've asked them verbally or nonverbally.

Many years ago I had a wonderful stress management course that I used to listen to on tape in the car when I was driving to work. The trainer called the things that make you feel off-balance 'leg lifters'. Go on, try this with someone you trust. Stand up with both feet planted squarely on the floor. Ask them to gently try to push you over. Now lift 1 foot and ask someone to push you again. Was it easier to push you over when you're fully grounded with both feet on the floor or when you only had 1 foot down? Life provides us with lots of leg lifters as we go, so you need to find the things that make you feel stable, safe, and grounded. When you find out what these are make sure you do them regularly.

As well as time for the child to be on their own, and time for ourselves, we need time together as a family. Ideally, this will be away from or situations that normally cause you stress and anxiety. Lots of children enjoy board games or computer games and there's no reason why you shouldn't do those with them, just bear in mind that you don't have to win. Know your family, and know what works for them. In our household for example, we don't play chess because I hate losing! We have loved playing card games, and have created family stories out of things that happened whilst we played. Laughter is the glue that holds the family together. Like the time I served freshly steamed broccoli with dinner only to find that it was so fresh there was a lightly steamed creature in the portion on one of the plates. Extra protein from the 'Caterpillar Cook'!

If at first you don't succeed – fail forward faster!

Sometimes we all get things wrong. One Christmas, we planned a present for the children. We wrapped the list of the things that they would have to take for a surprise holiday. They would need swimming costumes, towels, warm clothing, gloves and bicycles. We wrapped the list inside a matchbox inside a bigger box inside a slightly bigger box wrapped in 'S' shaped polystyrene packing inside a big box. Wrapped it in Christmas paper and label it to both of them. They opened the present on Christmas morning to much excitement, and a bit of confusion. On Boxing Day, we got up early, got the children in the car and set off. Our youngest kept asking where we were going and we wouldn't tell him. This went on over and over and over again until we arrived at a service station he was literally bouncing off the walls, so we decided to tell him then what we were going to do and where we were going to be. After that, he calmed down slightly but it wasn't until we had arrived at our accommodation, found his bedroom, unpacked, eaten and slept that he was able to calm down and begin to enjoy the holiday. If only we had known then how anxious he was, we would have prepared very differently!

Every time we fail, we have learnt something we didn't know before. As a parent I fail often. I take great comfort in the fact that I'm modelling what it is like to be an imperfect human being, so my children don't feel they have to be perfect. For their emotional and mental well-being it is really important that they can cope with things going wrong. If this is a challenge for your children I strongly suggest that you provide lots of opportunities for them to fail in a safe supportive and loving environment at home. The best teachers I have seen intentionally made mistakes on the board, so they can show students it's ok to get things wrong.

Many of us obsess over things that went badly. We replay the scene over and over again in our minds and find it hard to think about anything else. In my experience, tiredness makes it harder to avoid negative thoughts. Do what helps you to relax. The golfer, Jack Nicklaus said that "concentration is a fine antidote to anxiety." Becoming totally absorbed in a special interest, a favourite TV programme, or a book is a great way to move on.

Friends can be your family too

Not everyone has wonderful supportive family locally available on tap, but that doesn't mean you have to live without anyone to talk to. You might find help at your local church or other religious group or through friends you met at a baby and toddler group. There are specific organisations that are set up to provide support for families with disabilities. Often a web search will help you find these best. In the UK, Contact a Family[79] can link together families with specific disabilities and there are a number of charities specifically set up to support autistic people such as the National Autistic Society[80] which has a number of local branches, Ambitious about Autism,[81] and local autism organisations, many of whom are members of the Autism Alliance.[82] You may be given details of support groups at the point of diagnosis which can be helpful.

Although you are going to make lots of new friends, don't forget your old friends, some of whom will have known your child all of their life. They are ideally placed to help spot the triumphs that your child is having on the way to adulthood, especially when you're too close to see it.

You can't have the same qualitative relationship with friends online as you can in the flesh, but many people find friends on specialist forums for parents of children with disabilities. There is something hugely supportive about talking to someone who is going through, or has been through almost exactly the same issues that you are. Their experience will be slightly different to yours, especially if they're in a different part of the country, but it can certainly give you a different perspective, help you to pick up new ideas and a give you somewhere to

79 www.cafamily.org.uk

80 www.autism.org.uk

81 www.ambitiousaboutautism.org.uk

82 www.autism-alliance.org.uk

start if you're uncertain. You might like to try 'Talk about Autism',[83] or for other conditions look for moderated discussion boards. On Twitter or Facebook you can follow someone if you like what they say, which means that you automatically get anything they post. I have found some wonderful resources and really supportive comments on twitter, but I intentionally ignore negative sources.

It may not work for everyone, but it works for us!

Families are weird. Some families are weirder than others! It doesn't matter at all what happens in anyone else's household, feel free to do in your own home with your own family things that work for all of you. (Provided it is legal, decent, honest, truthful, not harmful and preferably fun!) So if that means that you communicate to each other by email that's fine. If it means that you all wear super soft clothing as you can't bear clothes to be scratchy and have a preference for a particular brand of fabric conditioner then that's fine too. If it doesn't bother you to have someone rolling around the floor in the middle of the TV programme then let the good times roll!

There are so many places in life that you just can't do what you need, where the physical space doesn't allow it, or other people just don't get why it matters. Your own home doesn't need to be like this. It can be tailored to the particular needs that your family have. It can be a place of safety and a refuge. It is the physical expression of the love that you have for your family, so allow it to wrap you in loving care.

---

83 www.talkaboutautism.org.uk

Chapter 8

Perfect Schools Don't Exist. How to Find the Best You Can

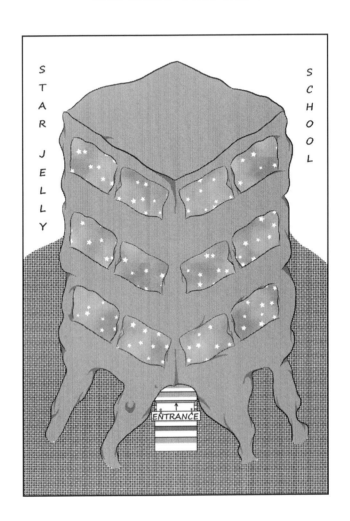

Know your child

One of the most difficult decisions a parent will ever make is deciding where to send their child to school. We all just want the best things for our children, but what 'best' is for that child isn't always easy to work out. How can you know this small person who is new, unformed and incomplete? How do you look forward in time to the person that they will be by the time they leave the school you are looking at now? This is particularly difficult when your child has special needs. In some ways, the more severely affected that they are, the easier the decision becomes. If your child is profoundly affected, and is preverbal, they will already be known to a range of support services and you will be given more help to identify specialist support. It is another one of those times when early diagnosis, and early intervention can be incredibly helpful in providing the right level of support at the right time.

If your child is verbal and of average ability or higher, then your issues tend to be slightly more complicated. Although intellectually they may fit brilliantly well into a mainstream school or nursery, there will be areas where their difficulties would be helped by accessing specialist support. How much of that is available in mainstream will depend very much from school to school and early years setting to setting. As well as their academic and educational needs, many of our children are very socially and emotionally vulnerable. As a result, it may be far better to find a setting emotionally supportive to them and strong on providing a nurturing, caring and supportive environment.

The other dimension to consider is the physical environment they will be in. If your child is on the autism spectrum for example, and has profound sensory needs so could not cope in a loud, busy environment, you might want to look for somewhere that is smaller, has more space, or is in a quieter setting. Of course this might not be possible. A school with a less than ideal environment but the understanding, flexibility and attitude to make the adjustments your child needs could still work better than one with the most beautiful environment that is unwilling to work with you.

The best in the area might not be the best for you

Many schools nowadays are judged on their position in league tables, as well as exam results, what other parents say about that school and the reputation that it has (whether deserved or not). A school's reputation is rarely the most up-to-date and accurate view of what a school really is like for a child when they're in it. Be especially wary of schools in very competitive areas. Results at the school might be affected as much by external coaching, tutoring, and the investment that parents make, as they are by the teaching that happens within the school. It can be very easy to get caught up in trying to do the best for your child academically, but if your child learns in a non-standard way, they might need a more personalised solution to help them succeed.

I know parents who become hugely emotionally invested in whether their child does or doesn't get into a particular school, especially if the school is thought to be the best in the area. The emotional pressure on the child is corrosive. By putting so much emphasis on academic performance, we run the risk of undermining the fact that all people have value and that individual effort makes far more difference in the long run than natural talent. One teacher told me of the really distressing scenes in school the day after the test results came out that decided which school a group of 11 year old children would go to. The children who failed to get in were upset, and some of the children who did get in were crowing and being mean to the same children who had been their best friends just the day before. There will always be a shuffling of alliances at this stage, but it is just a phase they go through.

Let's face it, you do not have an average child, or you would not be reading this book. So you need to consider very carefully the profile of your child, what you know about them, and how this matches the options that are open to you. We are looking for the right place for the child you have, not the school that you want to go to, or the one that was like the school that you went to when you were younger, but the one that will bring out the unique skills, abilities, and value in your child.

Balancing social and emotional with educational and academic needs

How on earth can you decide what is most important? What if there is a school that you know will meet your child's needs emotionally, or their sensory needs, but won't give them the academic opportunities that you feel they need? Do you send them to a school that prizes academic performance, because you know they are capable of it, but worry that the pace of the lessons and the academic pressure might be too much for them?

Making the choice can be difficult, especially so when you are looking at your schooling through the lens of someone who has very specific needs. The psychologist, Abraham Maslow[84] suggested that there is a hierarchy of needs that each individual has which must be satisfied before they can value anything in the level above. He was thinking about adults, but we need to bear in mind that our children become adults as they grow, whatever level they function at.

1. **Biological and physiological needs** – air, food, drink, shelter, warmth, physical attraction, sex, sleep, etc.

2. **Safety needs** – protection from elements, security, order, law, limits, stability, etc.

3. **Social needs** – Belongingness and Love, – work group, family, affection, relationships, etc.

4. **Esteem needs** – self-esteem, achievement, mastery, independence, status, dominance, prestige, managerial responsibility, etc.

5. **Cognitive needs** – knowledge, meaning, etc.

6. **Aesthetic needs** – appreciation and search for beauty, balance, form, etc.

7. **Self-Actualisation needs** – realizing personal potential, self-fulfilment, seeking personal growth and peak experiences.

8. **Transcendence needs** – helping others to achieve self-actualisation.

---

84 Maslow, A. H. (1970a). *Motivation and Personality*. New York: Harper & Row.

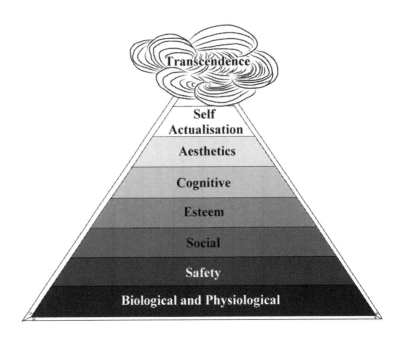

We can use this model as a possible way of helping us to decide which of our child's conflicting needs we should prioritise, bearing in mind that everyone is different and that your child might value something else far higher. If I had to choose between a school where I felt that my child would be safe, or one that was beautifully maintained, I would choose the place of safety. So many children with special needs are emotionally vulnerable, that I would prioritise a school with strong pastoral support. I do not believe that a child can learn well in a school where they feel under threat, whether that is from other students or teachers. If in doubt, think through what the impact will be on the child when they are grown up. Happiness and mental health trumps academic results for me every time.

When is a special school the right choice?

Making a decision like this is an important one for your family and it has to work for you. There are several things you need to be aware of. Special schools are not all the same. What children do they currently have in the school? How many of them have the same condition as your child? Do they have severe learning disabilities, are they designated for moderate learning difficulties or do they specialise in behavioural emotional and social difficulties? Special schools have fewer pupils, higher staff ratios, and sometimes (but not always) better specialist facilities. Do they have specific expertise in particular learning difficulties? Is this an autism specific special school? Does it cater especially for children with dyslexia or developmental coordination disorder? Given that the population within the school changes, and that the needs for special school places will vary over time, school designations change. Probably more important is to know what training the members of staff within the school have. Get to know what qualifications apply for the condition that your child has, and what training is generally well-regarded.

Special schools are expensive to run, and have more staff per pupil than in mainstream. They cost more per head which means that unless your child really cannot manage within a mainstream environment (or more probably that mainstream schools can't cope with them), they will not be offered a place at a special school. Some special schools are funded by the government, through the local authority or school board, whilst others are set up and run by individuals, companies, or charities. The National Autistic Society in the UK, for example, owns and runs seven autism specific special schools. The NAS also runs a system of accreditation separately for schools. For dyslexia and other specific learning difficulties, it is worth seeing if the school is registered by the Council for the Registration of Schools Teaching Dyslexic Pupils (CReSTeD).[85]

Most pupils are funded to attend schools by the local authority where they live. Some young people are lucky enough to have a specialist school placement that is suitable and close enough to where they live for them to attend daily. But a 2006 report from the Autism Education Trust[86] found that children with high functioning autism and significant mental health needs or behavioural problems that cause

---

85 Find CReSTeD at www.crested.org.uk

86 *Educational provision for children and young people on the autism spectrum living in England: a review of current practice, issues and challenges* Autism Centre for Education and Research University of Birmingham. November 2008 Research Team, Dr Glenys Jones, Annette English, Karen Guldberg, Professor Rita Jordan, Penny Richardson, Dr Mitzi Waltz

themselves injury or otherwise cause concern, were far more likely to be placed in residential care out of the local authority and often a long distance away from their families.

Given how expensive this type of provision is, and how difficult it is for young people to live away from home when there are significant special needs, it is usually better for young person to be included in a mainstream setting close to home provided that it is suitable for their needs. Since the report was written in 2006, there has been an increase in the number of specialist units attached to mainstream schools in the UK. Set up as a halfway house between mainstream and special, autism resource bases can provide specialist support whilst maintaining strong links with the wider school community. Considerable efforts have been made to improve the level of training, awareness, and understanding of staff in mainstream schools. The UK government funded the development of the Inclusion Development Programme (IDP)[87] which provides online training and professional development in autism, speech language and communication needs, dyslexia and behaviour, emotional and social difficulties. There is an IDP program for primary and secondary school staff, and an additional set of resources in each area for staff working in the early years (age 0-5). It also funded the development of a programme of training, standards and professional competencies in autism through the Autism Education Trust (AET)[88] for early years, schools and post 16 settings. The AET have trained over 50,000 people since 2012.

What makes a good setting?

The slightly glib answer is one that meets your child's needs! There are several features though, that will help you to decide whether what you're looking at is good. Watch how the staff react to the children, see if you can imagine your child there. If in doubt, trust your instinct; after all, you know your child best.

1. Do they have high expectations that are realistic?

2. Are all staff well-trained to understand your child's specific

---

87 www.idponline.org.uk

88 www.autismeducationtrust.org.uk

difficulties? To what level and is the training recognised or accredited?

3. Are they are accessible and do they communicate well with families?

4. Do the children make progress academically, socially and emotionally?

5. Do the children look happy and engaged in what they are doing?

6. Are the children learning skills that will help them as adults or are the staff only interested in getting them through exams?

7. Is the approach to young people professional, thoughtful and caring?

8. Are they accredited by a disability-specific body?

So much depends on the environment that the school creates within its walls. All staff should have a good awareness of the conditions of the children who are within their care. That includes office staff, midday supervisors, governors, teaching assistants and anybody working in the school. The best schools provide this awareness for people in the outside community as well, so that when their students go out they are welcomed rather than ostracised.

What your child's teachers need you to know

Teachers don't get up early every morning, work flat-out during the day, go home exhausted then work late into the evening to do a bad job. I have heard teachers talk of having no time to go to the toilet, no time to eat lunch and buying materials out of their own pocket for their classes to use when there are no funds available. They are, for the most part, an amazingly committed, passionate, energetic and caring bunch who went into teaching to help children learn and develop. They didn't go into teaching to make your child miserable, unhappy, and frustrated. If that is what is happening then something is going wrong, and it might not be totally down to the staff. Teachers seem to be under increasing administrative pressure and are almost as tested and monitored as our children. Before you go steaming into school as an enraged parent asking for an explanation, it might help to remember that.

If someone marched up to me tomorrow aggressively and asked me what I was going to do about something that had happened, I wouldn't feel inclined to sort it out. If on the other hand, the same person came up to me and said, "we have a problem because this is going on. What can we do to sort this problem out and how can I help?" then I would feel far more inclined to want to investigate and find a solution. Your child needs you to work with their teacher to resolve any issues that they face.

Start with the end you want to achieve in mind. Then you can work backwards from there and come up with ideas as to how you as a team can make it happen. For example, you are called into school because your child is refusing to go into the canteen for lunch. Sit down with the teacher, and between you work out whether eating lunch in the canteen is an important thing for your child to do, and if it is, how you can go about helping them to do it. It may be that your young person finds the canteen too noisy. If that is the case, maybe she could go in 15 minutes earlier or at the end of lunch (provided food could be put aside for her) when it is quieter or eat somewhere else altogether.

Nowhere is perfect all of the time

No matter how good the school is, there will always be problems that crop up along the way. Much as we would like them to be miniature carbon copies of perfectly behaved model members of society, our children are work in progress (just like us) and will get things wrong! Sometimes even the most experienced teacher can get a situation wrong and cause upset. Or another child will take exception to yours and may bully your child. Whatever the problem, the first stage of sorting it out is open communication.

What do you do if your child comes home in a really bad mood, behaves differently, or is silent and withdrawn? When you manage to talk to them they say some things that really worry you about the school. You might think you know what is happening, but you might be wrong – especially in the case of children on the autism spectrum, whose understanding of what has happened in a social context might not be correct. Whilst it absolutely expresses what they understand has happened, other people might see the same situation very differently. Then again, they may be being bullied. It's important to listen with an open mind to your child and gather all the facts without causing them any more distress.

The next stage is to go into the school as soon as you can and talk through what has been said. Try to avoid making assumptions and listen openly. If what you were told doesn't match what you believe to be the case you will have to judge whether it sounds likely from what you know about your child. If it doesn't make any sense to you, feel free to use examples where your child's behaviour was very different to what you've been told saying, "that's surprising, because when…" Once you have agreed what will happen next, write it down and don't forget to follow up any actions you promised to do.

When to carry on working with the school and when to move on

It's so easy to get into a negative cycle when your child is having difficulties in school and to let that affect how you see the school and everything it offers. Bear in mind that it isn't always the right decision to move the child. Most children don't like change, and would prefer to stay put than to move. It also depends how badly the situation is affecting them, how old the child is and how close they would be to leaving in any event. Check whether moving the child will solve the problem. Unless an alternative placement can provide a real benefit, a safer or more specialised approach for your child then the chances are that the problems will just move with them. If your child is being bullied, you move them and they are bullied again in the second school it will feel worse for them. The most effective interventions address the unacceptable behaviour of the bully and work to make the victim less vulnerable to bullying at the same time.

The first port of call always has to be to try to work with the school where you are, but sometimes that will just not be possible. If you have tried everything you can and are in danger of becoming confrontational, it can be really helpful to take someone else in with you for discussions with the school. In the UK, this may be someone from the local Information Advice and Support Service,[89] or it could be a family friend or another professional. If the school cannot or will not do anything to change the situation, I would recommend moving the child.

It can be very difficult to get your child into another state school when so many are oversubscribed and there are no spare school places. I do know of one girl who hated her school so much she tried to get out of a moving car. Her mother rang every school in the area and managed to find a private school who offered her a place for the 18 months until secondary school and a bursary to help cover the cost. In the UK, you do have the right to withdraw your child from state education and educate them at home. However, if you do so, the local authority no longer has an obligation to provide education for your child unless your child has a Statement of SEN or Education Health and Care Plan (EHCP). If your child refuses to attend school, but you have not withdrawn them, the local authority is still obliged to provide your child with an education.

Helping a child who is really unhappy

Miserable children make parents unhappy too. Our natural inclination is to do anything to make the child's pain go away. But sometimes that's beyond our ability to solve. It's even worse when we can't work out what the problem is, if the child has difficulty communicating with us, or is just too distressed to do so. Few children can explain what's going on when they're in the maelstrom of emotions. So do whatever helps them to calm down, and tell you what is going on. Some people find that drawing a cartoon of what happened works, because it doesn't needs lots of words to explain. Another approach is to use Playmobile characters or Lego mini figures to act out what happened.

Once you know the cause, you're able to start thinking what you could do. You might help the child to think of other ways that they could

---

89 IAS Services have a duty to provide information, advice and support to disabled children and young people, and those with SEN, and their parents. They are statutory services which means there has to be one in every local authority. (See www. iassnetwork.org.uk for details)

have behaved in a particular situation. Or it may be that you need to go and talk to the school, or nursery about the incident. Some children with autism find it really difficult to work out what has upset them. They may be distressed by a change of routine, a new teacher in the class, a different route into school, or the introduction of new for food for example.

Whatever the problem, you need to find a safe space where they can feel relaxed, calm, and happy. So if they have a special interest make sure that they have time to do that. Many children like videogames, or playing with trains, others like to research Otis lifts or other niche subjects. In the same way that exercise is helpful for you, it can also be helpful for them. A walk in the open air, a bike ride, a swing in the park, a trampoline in the garden, a punch bag in their room; chance to use Play-Doh, Plasticine or clay can all be helpful. Sometimes, time watching their favourite television programme or making something will do the trick. Find what they love, what calms them down, makes them feel safe, and do it. They'll love you for it.

The terror of transition

We all worry about going somewhere new and trying something different. But for lots of children with special needs, this can be a period of extreme anxiety and fear. Children have to deal with change throughout their lives, but detailed planning of how this is going to happen and a well thought through transition plan can act like magic in helping them to feel safe, secure, and welcome in the new setting. Some useful guides on easing the path for children moving from one place to another are available from The Autism Education Trust,[90] and the Transition Information Network.[91]

We can prepare for many of the big changes that happen. We know the children will go to school, they will move from primary to secondary and they will have to leave school to go on to college, university or to go onto residential care as an adult. It helps to know your destination

---

90 Autism Education Trust Transition Toolkit: http://autismeducationtrust.org.uk/resources/transition%20toolkit.aspx

91 Transition Information Network: http://councilfordisabledchildren.org.uk/transition-information-network/information-and-support/transition-guides

in advance. When you know where you're going, you can take pictures of it, introduce your young person to where they will be and sometimes even their teacher or teaching assistant or the Learning Support department at college. There is some fantastic practice around transition. At my children's school for example, there was a transition day when all children across the County go to visit their new school. The new school gave them a booklet that with all the information they needed to know in advance. It had a map, photos of all the Year 7 teachers, a sample timetable, lunch menus, uniform rules and who to go to for help. This was done for ALL students in the school.

Some schools have transition guides produced by young people themselves. One group of year seven students in an autism special school prepared an induction DVD for year six students who would be joining the school in September. They got to show students the school, and introduce them to the things that they found overwhelming initially. The DVD included things that members of staff might not have thought could cause a problem. It is good practice for any student who might find transition difficult to be offered additional visits to their new school setting. Ideally, this will also include an opportunity to talk to the SENCO about any issues that are worrying them. Having a booklet, or a DVD to take away has the advantage that the child can be shown that again over the long summer holiday to remind them where they will be going and increase their familiarity and therefore how comfortable they feel in the new setting. If in doubt, think visits and visuals.

Nothing lasts forever – moving on

School is only one part of life, and children to grow up into adults. This can be particularly scary for young people who do not want or like change. Some young people really struggle with adolescence, identify with their body as a child, and reject the image of themselves when it changes. All children struggle with their identity, but it is especially difficult when they can't understand the changes that are happening to their own body. They need to be taught explicitly, using accurate language and clear description the changes that their body will go through. There is a detailed fact sheet available from the National

Autistic Society[92] which explains how to talk about puberty with a young person on the spectrum. The FPA (formerly Family Planning Association) produces a series of books that are not autism–specific but for people with learning difficulties.[93]

It is really important that children with special needs are taught about sex and relationships using tangible real examples that make sense. If you tried to teach a young person with autism that they need to use a condom to prevent infections and pregnancy, for example, and demonstrate by putting the condom onto a cucumber then you cannot be surprised when some young people think putting condoms on cucumbers is a method of birth control! There are anatomically correct educational models that teachers can buy that look like a real penis, which is far more helpful, especially for children who are very literal.

We also need to think about the role of lifelong learning. The teenage brain doesn't mature until the age of 25. In the case of young people with special needs, they may be operating at a lower level of emotional maturity for some time longer. Most skills take longer to learn and may well need to be taught explicitly, whereas children who develop in a neurotypical way will pick up those skills naturally. We need to look at the skills that children need for life, whether they are around sex and relationships, using public transport, or managing money. All of these need to be taught, and are just as important as academic goals.

92 http://library.autism.org.uk/Portal/Default/en-GB/RecordView/Index/14647

93 *Talking together...about growing up* by Kerr-Edwards and Scott (2010);
Talking together about sex and relationships by Kerr-Edwards and Scott (2010b);
Talking together about contraception by Kerr -Edwards and Scott (2010c)

Chapter 9

Bullying, Vulnerability and Resilience

Why are children like ours so vulnerable?

We all want our children to be safe. Whether we are talking about being safe physically, mentally, on the street, or online, we need to feel that they're going to be ok. There are a number of issues affecting the safety of children with SEN. They are far more likely to become victims of bullying than their neurotypical peers. There are a number of reasons why this would be the case. It is human nature to fear difference, so we need to teach everyone that difference is ok.

Children with autism and ADHD often find it difficult to control the impulses they feel. Many of them definitely come from the act first, think later brigade and in common with many young people they lack the higher-level thinking skills that help them assess in advance whether something is a good idea to do or not. Add that to the difficulties that young people experience in understanding how to have a conversation, how to take turns, how to 'get' jokes, dealing with and understanding the way that non-verbal communication works, and you have a recipe for disaster. All children in this age group are vulnerable if they are alone. The good news is that just one friend can protect a child from bullying.

You might notice the young people who are confident are rarely the ones who are picked on. Positive experiences build confidence, self-assurance, and positive self-esteem. Unfortunately, that isn't the experience for everyone. Children who find things difficult at school will have experienced failure again and again. If they are aware of those around them, they will notice that others don't have the same problems. Many children with dyslexia for example, will do almost anything to avoid writing, because they know this is difficult and because they know they will fail at it, and hate feeling stupid. If we failed at something over and over again, we wouldn't feel confident either.

Good friends, bad friends and manipulation

We all want our children to have good friends who are great to spend time with, but the reality is rather more complicated for many of us. If your child mentions someone else's name just once, there is a temptation to seize on it immediately and leap into sorting out play dates, food, activities, in fact anything that will add to the event. Relationships take time to grow, and time to develop between children just as they do with adults. More than once, I have leapt in too early and found that it just didn't work. Whilst the children are very small it's fine, but as they get older they need to do things on their own terms and learn how to do it themselves, however difficult that may be for them.

If we are going to be in the position where we trust them to make decisions about their friends (which we should be doing if at all possible), then we need to explicitly teach our children what makes a good friend and what makes a bad friend. They need to know that a good friend is someone who looks out for you and helps you to be the best person you can be. It takes a really good friend to tell you when you are wrong and help you to do better. Some of our children's friends though, are a less than positive influence. If someone is constantly getting your child into trouble, or is behaving in a way that makes them miserable, then they are by definition not a good friend.

What do you do then if your child only has one friend, or they really like them, and you really don't? After all, you can't choose their friends for them much as you might like to. There isn't much you can do other than to give your child as many opportunities to meet different people and find individuals with whom they are likely to have things in common. This is another example of where your child's special interest can be a real benefit. Some children have loved being part of the Pokémon club, or playing Warhammer at school at lunchtime. Try lots of things and see what they love.

What is bullying?

Every child is different, and their ability to deal with social stresses varies from one person to the next, so it can be very hard to know when your child is upset and reporting something that happened at school, whether it is just part of the natural rough-and-tumble of the school environment or if they are actually being bullied. Young Minds[94] is an organisation that helps young people maintain good levels of mental

94 www.youngminds.org.uk

health. Their definition of bullying is "…where someone hurts you either physically, by hitting or kicking you, or verbally by calling you names or teasing you." They list a number of behaviours that might be bullying. They include:

- name-calling and teasing

- spreading lies

- pushing and pulling, hitting, kicking and causing physical pain

- taking money or possessions

- excluding from activities

- threatening and intimidating

- texting horrible messages

- filming on mobile phones and spreading it about

- sending horrible emails or messages on Facebook or other social networking sites.

Some people are bullied because they are gay, for the colour of their skin, because they are fat or skinny, because of their gender, because they are disabled or simply because they're different. It is never acceptable.

It can be hard to know from outside the situation whether or not a child is being bullied. There can be a pretty fine line between banter and bullying. Most widely accepted definitions accept that bullying has to be:

1. Deliberate

2. Malicious

3. Repeated

Sometimes a child is too scared to tell anybody in case bullying gets worse, or they might feel they deserve it or are somehow responsible for what they are experiencing. The NSPCC[95] suggests a number of

95 www.nspcc.org.uk

signs you might notice if the child:

- has their belongings taken or damaged

- is over-tired and hungry from not eating lunch (if their dinner money or lunch has been taken)

- is afraid to go to school, is mysteriously 'ill' each morning, or skips school

- suffers a drop in performance at school

- asks for, or steals, money (to pay someone else)

- is afraid of travelling on the school bus or on their own to school

- is nervous, loses confidence, or is distressed

- stops eating or sleeping

- begins to bully others

- refuses to say what's wrong or is withdrawn

- is physically injured.

The Institute of Education at the University of London in a recent report[96] found that children with special educational needs and disabilities were more than twice as likely to be bullied as other children in primary school. The impact of bullying can be devastating for the child in the short term and the long term. Children who are bullied at school are more likely to have low self-esteem, anxiety, and depression during adulthood.[97] They may not do as well in terms of their overall achievement. They are at greater risk of developing an

96 Stella Chatzitheochari, Samantha Parsons & Lucinda Platt. Bullying experiences among disabled children and young people in England: Evidence from two longitudinal studies. *Institute of Education*. London, 2014.

97 Arseneault, L, Bowes, L and Shakoor, S (2010) Bullying Victimization in Youths and Mental Health Problems: "Much Ado about Nothing"? *Psychological Medicine* 40(5): 717–729; Bond, L, Carlin, J, Thomas, L., Rubin, K and Patton, G (2001) Does Bullying Cause Emotional Problems? A Prospective Study of Young Teenagers. *British Medical Journal* 323: 480–484; Takizawa, R, Maughan, B and Arseneault, L (2014) Adult health outcomes of childhood bullying victimization: Evidence from a 5-decade longitudinal British birth cohort. *American Journal of Psychiatry* (Online First); Wolke, D, Copeland, W, Angold, A and Costello, J (2013) Impact of Bullying in Childhood on Adult Health, Wealth, Crime, and Social Outcomes. *Psychological Science* 24(10): 1958–1970.

eating disorder such as anorexia or bulimia, truant from school or having suicidal thoughts.[98]

Before you panic though, it is important to remember that lots of children experience behaviours that are bullying at some stage in their childhood. These may not be sustained, severe or have long-term impact if they are a one-off and are dealt with appropriately at the time. A certain amount of jostling for position and rough-and-tumble is normal within the school environment, and as parents we want to build resilience in our children so that when bad things happen to them they know how to deal with them without it shaking their belief in themselves as worthwhile people. It crosses a line if a child becomes seriously upset, is injured or is the victim of systematic and continued bullying. That is when you need to get help.

Protecting your children online

Sometimes it can feel like the Wild West out on the Internet, and whilst it's a great place to find all sorts of information help, support, and friendships, there are some people, places and actions that are not safe. So how on earth do you know how to support your child unless you're a super techie and are more at home on the Internet than they are? Some schools are fantastic and will provide training for parents in cyber safety appropriate for primary and secondary age children. If it's on offer, take it!

In the same way that you teach your child to cross the road, we also need to teach them how to protect themselves from other people, and how they should behave themselves. Talk to them about what is acceptable to say online, and explain that they shouldn't say anything online they wouldn't say in person or that they wouldn't feel comfortable saying in front of you (or an authority figure if your parenting style is very informal)! The Child Exploitation and Online Protection Centre

98   Nansel, T, Overpeck, M, Pilla, R, Ruan, W, Simons-Morton, B and Scheidt, P (2001) Bullying Behaviors among US youth: Prevalence and Association with Psychosocial Adjustment. *The Journal of the American Medical Association* 285(16): 2094–2100.
Rigby, K and Slee, P (1993) Dimensions of Interpersonal Relation among Australian Children and Implications for Psychological Well-being. *The Journal of Social Psychology* 133(1): 33–42

(CEOP) has a fantastic website[99] which gives specific advice for parents based on whether your child is in primary or secondary school.

Cyberbullying

If your child is being bullied online what should you do? First, reassure them and make sure they are ok, then talk to your child and gather evidence around what happened and whether they know who it is. Go to the child's school as issues often spill over into the school environment. Then go to the provider of the website or the phone company and report the incident. That enables them to remove the content and block the bullies so the young person doesn't have to experience any more bullying.

Grooming

Grooming is where people with a sexual interest in children contact them in order to get them to do sexual acts either over the Internet or in person. The Internet is a wonderful place to make friends who are interested in similar things but some sex offenders use social networking sites, chat rooms and games to befriend children and build a relationship with them, sometimes by pretending to be someone else. Your best defence is to keep an open relationship with your child, be aware of which sites they are using and what they're doing with those people online and whether they know them in the real world. Encourage them to come to you if they feel at all uncomfortable about anything that someone says to them online. If you think your child is going out to meet someone right now who they met online, you do not know and haven't met, this is an emergency, ring 999 immediately.

Politically and sexually inappropriate websites

Whilst there are some amazingly good and helpful websites on the Internet, it also hosts sites which hold extreme attitudes that many people find difficult as adults, and that children are really not ready or able to understand. The first stage is to set age appropriate controls on the sites that your children are able to access through all of their Internet enabled devices. Many providers have free parental control packages,

---

99 www.thinkuknow.co.uk/parents from Child Exploitation and Online Protection (CEOP) Centre.

but other software is available to block access to adult websites such as pornographic and gambling sites. Whilst the use of pornography by young teenage boys is common and developmentally normal, it is easy online to access a wide variety of pornographic content which includes hard-core and extreme images and videos. Pornography rarely shows sex as a part of a natural loving relationship, and there is mounting concern that early exposure to hard-core pornography can give young people inaccurate and unhealthy views about the opposite sex and what they can expect from them. This is always going to be a difficult and embarrassing conversation for parents and children, which is why it is really important to have it and to be as open as possible.

Losing control of images

Most of us have seen photographs we don't like which we are largely able to destroy. What is changed in recent years is how quickly pictures and videos can be copied shared and spread at great speed. A picture taken to share between friends can easily end up in the hands of someone that they don't trust. At a school briefing on cyber safety, the police told us of a teenage girl who took a completely suitable photograph of herself (a selfie) not knowing that her younger sister was in the background in her gym leotard. She sent the photo to friends, and it was found in the property of a sex offender. Once a picture is online it can leave the young person vulnerable to bullying or blackmail. It can be very difficult to remove, and can affect a young person's reputation in the long term. Pictures become part of the person's 'digital footprint' and can pop up if someone searches for their name before a job interview.

Sharing information online – managing an online reputation

The Internet is providing a permanent record of the highs and lows of a young person's thoughts, opinions and activities, but if these aren't controlled carefully they can be accessible to future employers, universities, or partners. Young people really need to think carefully about what they share, where they share it and who they share it with. The more information you share about yourself online, the easier it is for a stranger to build a picture about you, so check your child's privacy settings so that they can control what they share and who they share it with. There are specific threats if young person shares location information on themselves as it makes them vulnerable to abduction. No person under 18 should have location services switched on for any social network that they use.

Using mobile phones and tablets safely

Many young people feel their mobile phone is as much a part of them as breathing. Most devices now give access to the whole of the Internet including potentially inappropriate sites, so when setting up your child's phone or tablet make sure that you have age-appropriate settings switched on. Any device with a camera can be used for taking photos and videos which can be uploaded in the blink of an eye. Other people can easily use your child's phone. Consider setting a pin code or password so no one else has access to personal information, online accounts or can run up expensive bills. As with all personal information, young people should be careful who they give the number to. It can be really hard to get your child to surrender their phone for any period at all, but there is mounting research that looking at screens late at night disrupts sleep. Sleep deprivation has a negative effect on all of us, so consider removing phones and screens from bedrooms and charging them elsewhere at night. Finally make sure you know the unique number for their phone to contact to get the SIM card blocked. Make a note of the phone's unique 'IMEI' number (if you can't find the purchase details dial #06# on the phone). The police can then identify the phone if it has been stolen and turns up – though this seems to be rare. As someone who has had one phone stolen and dropped two into water (once down the toilet and once into the washing up bowl) I insure mine!

Anxiety and sensory differences

Children with different types of SEN often find life far harder and scarier than most. If you imagine a child who is anxious what do you see? If you are looking really closely you might notice they are quiet, or unusually loud, but their feelings and fears are internal. Like an iceberg, what you see in terms of behaviour is just the tip, most of what's going on within the child is happening under the waterline and can't be seen at all unless it is particularly severe. You might notice that your child reacts strongly to some things that happen far more than you would expect given the situation. This is usually an indication that something else is going on.

Most children on the autism spectrum have differences in their sensory perception. They might be either over or under sensitive to a particular sensory stimulus. It can affect all of their senses sight, sound, smell, touch, taste, balance, and body awareness. An individual can be sensory avoiding or sensory seeking. Some people can see fluorescent lights flickering which is very distracting, whereas most people won't notice. Some people are captivated by the flickering light and like shiny, sparkly objects. If you are very sensitive to touch for example and another child brushes past you in the corridor it might feel as if they've hit you. Some young people are very sensitive to sound and find the bustle and noise of a large school environment exhausting. Even if they cope with that really well whilst at school, they can be so overwhelmed that they 'kick off' when they get home. This is so common it is called the 3 o'clock time bomb. Sometimes teachers find it hard to believe that there is a problem with a particular student who behaves beautifully during the day and think that this child who is really difficult at home is due to poor parenting rather than them dealing with overwhelming sensory assault in a safe environment.

It is really helpful to complete a sensory profile with a child so that you're able to identify the things that they find intrusive difficult, and stressful and also to identify what they find calming and helpful. I know of young people who are calmed by touching something soft and so either wear very soft clothing under their uniform or carry a small square of their favourite material that they can touch that when they feel the need. Other young people use their iPods or phones with headphones to calm themselves using music. Once you have identified what sensory needs your young person has you can build that into their day and give them a mix of activities that meets their sensory needs.

Pain thresholds and sensory overload

People have widely varying pain thresholds but it has been widely documented that many young people with autism have a very different response to pain. One young man I know of broke his finger but gave no sign of pain or discomfort. It was only because his parents noticed that it was an unusual shape that he was taken to hospital x-rayed and treated. Other young people are so sensitive to touch that lightly brushing their skin is extremely painful.

If you want to know what overwhelm might feel like, let's imagine a day when everything goes wrong. The alarm doesn't go off, and you oversleep. You can't find what you want to wear, you knock over your cup of coffee and don't have time to eat anything before you run out the door. You get in the car, turn the key and start driving. Because you're late the traffic is much worse than normal so your journey takes you longer. You suddenly notice that you're running out of petrol and there isn't a garage that's easy to reach on the way to work. When you arrive, you find you have a meeting you've forgotten all about and it started half an hour ago. You walk into the meeting late and flustered. Everyone turned to look at you. How do you feel now? Are you able to concentrate on the details of the meeting? Some young people operate at that level of stress every day, and we still expect them to learn and respond in the same way as everyone else!

Imagine each different stimulus piling one of top of another. Each unwelcome sensory assault is like pouring water into a teacup. If you are calm, happy and relaxed, then your cup can take quite a bit of water before it overflows. On the other hand, if you're already anxious, the level of water in your teacup starts high and it takes less before it pours over the top. This is what we see when young people go into meltdown. If you want to begin to understand what this might feel like, there are some really good films available free on YouTube such as 'A is for Autism'.[100] The first thing children lose in any stressful situation is the ability to talk about what's going on clearly and concisely in a way that other people can understand. So keep calm, lower the volume, use fewer words and give your young person somewhere calm and quiet to regain their equilibrium.

Success, failure and the demon of perfectionism

Getting things wrong is a really difficult thing to accept in our modern day society. All you have to do is look in the papers and see people criticised for their mistakes, getting things wrong, and changing their

100 A.Is.For.Autism. (Tim Webb, 1992) YouTube.

minds. We tend to appreciate people who are steadfast, which is a great thing in terms of values, but a very poor way of living life. If we are afraid to try new things and afraid to grow, we risk cutting ourselves off from some of the best opportunities that are presented to us. I remember asking a Chief Executive why he appointed someone who had failed in a previous job. He told me that the manager had learnt more from his mistakes than we learn from success. Each and every human being has an amazing potential for growth regardless of where they start from. We never know what's going to happen in the future but we do know that having a positive approach in general and especially learning from our mistakes enables us to develop in ways that we would never have been able to predict.

If we find dealing with failure hard, our children will find it even harder. I know lots of children who will crumple up work if it doesn't meet their expectations, will scribble over something that's been criticised, and who will give up activities if they don't feel they're succeeding. Our job is to see, recognise, and support them through those feelings of frustration, anger and disappointment. It really doesn't help to tell anyone they shouldn't feel the way they do, but allowing them to feel that emotion, supporting them whilst they feel it and giving them a positive way out of that feeling helps the child not to get stuck in the maelstrom of scary emotions. So if your child is doing a drawing and it goes wrong and they getting upset about it and is scribbling it out so hard that the pencil rips the paper, you might try saying something like "oh dear, you looked really frustrated, did your drawing go wrong? It can be hard when things don't turn out how you planned. Let's go and do something else for a bit, you can have another go at a different drawing later."

One of the best techniques I've ever found, is to model a positive approach to failure myself. There are lots of opportunities to share with my children when I get things wrong! What I've noticed is that they have begun to adapt a far more flexible approach to things and get so much less stressed when things go wrong. We also like to take an analytical, problem solving approach to things that go wrong because it gives us distance from the difficult emotion of failure and into a frame of mind that rewards their resourcefulness at the same time as giving them credit for any positive actions that they take.

How to support healthy self-esteem in your child

I really hope that you've never had this experience, but if your child has come to you saying that it would be better to have never been born, the people in their class wish they didn't exist, or tell you that they want to kill themselves you will understand the importance of a child feeling valued. Without a sense of self-worth, children will seek reinforcement from anywhere, and that leaves them vulnerable to influence by people and places who don't have their best interests at heart. Time and again, adults who got into trouble as young people say that they were looking for a sense of who they were and of their value, but found it in all the wrong places. You can't control what anyone feels about themselves, but you can help to feed into a positive picture rather than a negative one.

There will be times when things don't go well for your child. No-one's journey is all joy and everyone needs to have some positive evidence to outweigh the negatives. I have mentioned before my 'glory file' which contains all of the certificates, positive letters, lovely cards and a hard copy of any emails that have said nice things about me. I'm fortunate in that I don't have people in my life who say lots of negative things to me, but I do have an internal critic who can be far more unpleasant than anyone else I would come across. I know a lot of children with SEN who have a very strong perfectionist streak and hate getting things wrong. They are their own worst critics, and need a balancing view so that they don't believe that they critic is right. Get them to collect pictures and images of the things that they are good at and the things that they love and put those right at the beginning of the glory file to set themselves in a positive context. On a bad day, they can be reminded to go and look at the glory file and accept that today was just a bad day, nothing lasts forever and tomorrow can be a better day.

We listen to the messages that we are told day in, day out. If those messages are all negative then what we believe about ourselves will be negative. If your child is struggling to be positive, then you need to supply that positive reinforcement for them. Catch them doing something right, anything right, and praise them for it. They are more likely to do positive things again; you'll get more of the behaviours that you want, and less of the ones you don't.

The failure factory and persistence – Edison, Bruce and other stories

"Opportunity is missed by most people because it is dressed in overalls and looks like work." – Thomas Edison

Inventor Thomas Alva Edison was born in Ohio USA in 1847.[101] He had scarlet fever and inner ear infections which left him with hearing difficulties in both ears. He was also a hyperactive child very prone to distraction. His family moved to Port Huron, Michigan, in 1854 where he went to school for a total of 12 weeks before his teacher found him 'difficult'. His mother, an accomplished school teacher, taught him at home where he showed a voracious appetite for knowledge and read books on a wide range of subjects. He is best known for the invention of the carbon filament light bulb in 1880 and founding the General Electric Company, holding more than 1000 patents for his inventions. He is widely credited with having a really positive attitude towards failure. It is hard to see how he would have been able to develop so much without his high level of energy and the support of his mother. He said of her, "My mother was the making of me. She was so true, so sure of me; and I felt I had something to live for, someone I must not disappoint."[102]

Learning resilience is really important. Things will and do go wrong, but if you can pick yourself up, dust yourself off and start all over again, you are much better fitted to cope with the ups and downs of life. There are lots of examples of resilience, from Robert the Bruce and the spider to Rudyard Kipling's poem, *If*, which includes the following:

If you can meet with Triumph and Disaster
And treat those two impostors just the same;
If you can bear to hear the truth you've spoken
Twisted by knaves to make a trap for fools,
Or watch the things you gave your life to, broken,
And stoop and build 'em up with worn–out tools

---

101   Thomas Alva Edison. [Internet]. 2014. The Biography.com website. Available from: http://www.biography.com/people/thomas-edison-9284349 [Accessed 29 Jun 2014].

102   Baldwin, Neal (1995). *Edison: Inventing the Century*. Hyperion. pp. 3–5. ISBN 978-0-7868-6041-8.

Persistence is an incredibly useful skill that needs to be practised on a regular basis and rewarded in our young people, especially in these times of instant gratification.

Peer awareness, peer mentoring and anti-bullying programs

There is only so much that we can do to help our children and fit them to be able to work in society. The best schools focus on accepting difference, make it a responsibility of all students to create a better environment for everyone, and do the same for the surrounding community. Within schools this can be done by running a peer awareness programme to teach pupils about difference and to understand that people have value irrespective of what they look like or how they behave. Peer awareness programmes generally have a positive impact on the amount of bullying that happens within a school, although clearly nothing will end it completely.

Peer awareness programs vary depending on the age and development of the children that you're working with. In infant schools, children are only just becoming aware that others are different to themselves so specialist programs like Woodfer's World from Ambitious about Autism are a good place to start.[103] When children get to the top of primary school, they tend to start jostling for position and forming groups in a different way. It is at this stage that we often see an increase in bullying. So for these slightly older children, in years 5, 6 and 7 (aged 9 to 12), the Autism Education Trust developed the 100% Awesomes,[104] a comic-based adventure delivered as a peer awareness lesson to a whole class. By the time they get to secondary school after the first year, programs that explain autism in more detail and give positive role models become really beneficial. Some Local Authority Outreach teams have specific peer awareness programmes they run. Nice examples include Hendon School (a large London mainstream school with an autism unit)[105] and Gareth D. Morewood's paper on

---

103 http://www.ambitiousaboutautism.org.uk/who-we-are/publications

104 www.autismeducationtrust.org.uk

105 www.advanced-training.org.uk/module1/M01U15.html from Advanced training materials for autism; dyslexia; speech, language and communication; emotional, social and behavioural difficulties; moderate learning difficulties developed for teachers and available through www.advanced-training.org.uk

'Mainstreaming Autism'.[106]

Peer mentors (without special needs) develop skills in listening, understanding, facilitating and supporting other people. Young people with SEN experience fewer incidences of bullying, develop better social skills, and are much happier and have a wider group of friends to call upon.

There is also an award-winning[107] whole-school anti-bullying programme from Finland called KiVa.[108] It was heavily supported and piloted by the Finnish government through randomized control trials (the gold-standard for research) and rolled out to 90% of all Finnish schools. The results in terms of minimising bullying are so impressive that it was piloted by the Welsh Government in 2012 as part of a programme led by Professor Judy Hutchings and Dr. Sue Evans at the University of Bangor.[109] What was most impressive was the significant reduction in victimisation and bullying reported by pupils.

Clubs and special interest groups

Think about your life as an adult and where you found the friends that you currently have; how did you meet? Where did your relationship start? And what have you got in common? I suspect that if you look at the origins of all of your friendships and relationships you will find that there is something that you share with the other person. For many women with children, this can be people they met in parenting class, postnatal group, or people who had children at the same nursery or school. Some of our friends come into our lives through hobbies, through things we love. It's no different for our children. They are more likely to find someone who sees the world in a similar way to them, if they share the same interests. It makes the difficult business of finding something to say far easier.

We talked earlier about the importance of special interests and following what people love to do. Lots of schools now have clubs at lunchtime

---

106 http://www.gdmorewood.com/wp-content/uploads/2015/05/G-Morewood-GAP-Article.pdf

107 Including the European Crime Prevention Award 2009.

108 www.kivaprogram.net is the KiVa website.

109 Training is available for schools through www.centreforearlyinterventionwales.co.uk

and after-school clubs that can follow their interests. These could be in any sort of subject. They could be clubs for maths, chess, debating, design and technology, music, choirs, orchestra, jazz band, wind band, guitar club, punk band, cinema, Minecraft, Warhammer, keep fit or running clubs. You name it, it could be available. Sometimes though, children won't join a club at school because the whole environment is too overwhelming. If they're having a really rough time with the children around them, it can be helpful to find a group that exists outside of the children they go to school with where that is possible. So maybe look for a Cub or Scout pack a little further away from home, where they can find new people they haven't had a problem with during the day. Of course, this doesn't mean they won't have any problems in that group, but it does at least give them a break from the personalities involved and gives them the potential to meet new people and possibly someone they like who likes them.

In these days of the internet it is so much easier to find activities outside school than it used to be, and many activities for adults have specialist youth sections for young people. Specialist schemes to develop young people in a number of sports, such as the paddle power scheme from the British Canoe union and the RYA schemes for sailors which operate through sailing clubs. You can pretty much pick your activity, and then find a club that does it, although you might have to travel to get there. If your child is less sporty, then look for other activities that you think they might enjoy and look for 'come and try' or open days. Some organisations have set up holiday play schemes, social groups, and youth clubs for young people with disabilities. There are also some specific social groups for teenagers with Asperger syndrome which have been life changing for the teens who attend.

It is worth remembering, though, that there is a balance to be struck between finding activities which your young person may come to love and providing down-time for them to rest and recover from the demands of social activities. Too many activities can lead to exhaustion, unhappiness and behaviours you would rather not have as a result of overwhelm. Don't forget to ask them and remember it's OK to drop activities if they stop being fun.

Understanding emotions, dealing with anger and frustration

Whilst typically developing children will learn to understand their emotions through absorbing and watching how other people behave, often children with special needs will need to be explicitly taught to identify, name and learn to deal with the emotions they feel. Many of our young people are highly volatile which is not at all surprising given the level of anxiety they are operating under and the stress caused by not being able to predict what will happen next.

If you know your young person really well, you can often predict or at least observe when things are going wrong, which gives you the opportunity to prevent it from spilling over into a full on meltdown. In the early stages, it can sometimes work to distract or divert the young person, whereas confrontation almost always just adds fuel to the fire, raises the emotional temperature, and triggers meltdown. One of the strategies that I have seen used, is for young people to be taught to recognise how their body feels when they're beginning to get angry, frustrated, or upset. Once you name it, you're far more likely to be able to tame it. Make the naming as tangible and personal to that individual as you possibly can, by using a photo and putting a label underneath it that says this is what my face looks like when I feel... and label the emotion. The next stage is to know what to do next. The Incredible Five-Point Scale[110] by Karrie Dunn Buron is a very visual tool that works by helping young people to identify, understand and rate the strength of their feelings. Once they can do that, you can work on appropriate responses to situations. Helping young people to be conscious of what helps them to feel calm, relaxed and happy, builds self-awareness and control. If your young person also has ADHD (hyperactivity type), then it can be quite important to include physical exercise in part of their daily routine as well as using it as a calming strategy.

---

110 www.5pointscale.com by Kari Dunn Buron.

Chapter 10

From Surviving To Thriving

Don't panic!

As we've gone through this book, we have learnt to celebrate and value the difference that our delightful, interesting, challenging, and rewarding children bring into our lives. Yes, there will be days when you don't know what to do, who to turn to, or how to solve the problems that you face. From time to time problems will be huge and your ability to solve them will feel very, very small. But that isn't the whole of the story. We are learning to recognise and use the wonderful tools, techniques and experiences of people who have already lived a lot of the issues that we face. Each person, each family, each situation has something new to teach us and if there's one thing that hitting rock bottom does, it makes us teachable. When we start to realise we don't have all the answers, is when we start to learn.

We are at a unique turning point in our history, when we have unprecedented access to other people, other experiences, and other ways of doing things that go far beyond our village, our region and even our country. For those of us with non-standard children this is the greatest gift we could ever be given. 'Our tribe' is out there, we can talk to each other, we can support each other and boy can we feel good! The first time we communicate with people who cannot speak, we start to learn how to understand them. People who are different are in a unique and valuable position. They can lead us by the hand into a world of wonder that we didn't know existed.

I want to see plays written by people who tell me something I don't already know, or express things in a way I haven't heard before. I want to look at pictures by painters who can see the world differently. I want to see with better eyes. To share their perspective, intention and emotion, especially when their experience is not my own. We all need engineers and scientists who see things from a different point of view. It is the dreamers who come up with new and innovative solutions to the problems we face today. I want young people with any of those skills to look at the situations we are in and feel their own sense of power in being able to come up with solutions, visions, and ideas for the future in their own inimitable way.

157

Change is scary but it can be good

Change is a natural and inevitable part of life that will happen whether or not we want it to. None of us like to feel uncomfortable, it makes us irritable, out of sorts, and scared. So being able to deal with, accept, and thrive in a context where things are altering all the time is a key life skill. Adding together little changes can enable us to feel more comfortable with the process. If we are going to grow, we need to practice accepting change to help us to become skilled at dealing with the unpredictable and cope with the big changes we can't control.

So much of life is all about context. How you look at any situation affects how you feel about it. I discovered early on, that when I imposed changes on my children without warning, things went wrong and we ended up arguing. We all hate being bounced into things. Giving them a choice between two things they didn't want to do was better than no choice at all. Such as, "Would you like to clean up your floor now, or after a drink?" Work out what could be changed and what is non-negotiable to give yourself more flexibility. Being able to choose between two good and helpful choices is a really useful life skill, as is not causing a confrontation you don't want.

Big life changes are the hardest to deal with. Having children, sending them to school for the first time, changing schools, leaving school, starting work and moving out are all difficult for everyone concerned. But these pale into insignificance when set against the impact of grief. If a parent, a sibling or a friend dies, it brings a change in our life we would never choose. Grief and loss are as inevitable as breathing, but occur so much less frequently, and are talked about less. I was struck by the story I heard on the radio of a man who went to interview people who had been survivors of the genocide in Rwanda. Whilst not underestimating for one moment the pain of the experiences they had been through, they all looked for something positive to come out of the experience. There can be moments of grace, and moments of joy even in the darkest places and at the darkest hours. Our job is to find them, and to teach our children how to find them too.

Doing the most difficult job in the world with deep joy

There is nothing easy about coping with lack of sleep night after night, week after week, month after month and sometimes year after year. Some people climb Everest, run marathons across the Sahara, or swim the Channel. I can't help feeling the only reason they're able to do those is because they aren't a parent! Sometimes, it's as much as we can do to get up, get everyone dressed, and get out of the house for school and work.

You will be called upon to find out things that you don't yet know, develop skills you don't have, and do things you never imagined you could. That you will be changed by the experience is as unavoidable as the wearing away of rock by a stream. It happens so slowly, you barely notice it, but look back years later and you will see the grooves, trace the path the water took, and feel the difference that it made. As a parent of a child with special needs, you have been invited to develop an understanding of difference, sensitivity to the needs of others, and appreciation of the people who travel alongside you bringing out the best in your child. How positive you are about the experience is up to you.

There is something hugely liberating in stepping aside from the values that a lot of society still holds. It's not better, not worse, just different. But when you can experience the full, solid and reliable conviction that there is beauty in everything, inner strength is yours for the asking. If you can see it clearly in your mind's eye, you can make it happen. I'm not talking about making the blind see and the lame walk, but I am talking about different ways of seeing and different ways of walking and what huge contribution each can bring to our lives.

Developing and modelling emotional resilience when things go wrong

Please don't get the mistaken impression that anyone manages to do this effectively all the time! Sometimes, when we are right at the top of our game, we planned everything effectively, anticipated a range of difficult situations and worked out what to do. We looked for resources and tools to help, found people we know who can help talk it through with us or take the strain themselves. We've joined communities of people who share similar situations, feelings and approaches. We try it, it works and we celebrate!

But life isn't always like that is it? I do believe that one of the worst things we can do to our children is to lead them to believe that everything will always be wonderful, because it won't. No matter how effective they are and how well they work or how hard they try, sometimes things just don't work out the way they want. We have to create an environment where it is okay to get things wrong and okay to fail from time to time. When you can accept that something has failed, use that failure to help you find other approaches you might try; failing can be good. Every problem is an opportunity to learn and grow if we choose to see it that way.

I don't mean for one minute that pretending that something isn't painful is helpful. There is real powerful in recognising, understanding, and experiencing a full emotion whether that is pain or joy. If you are really afraid to experience emotional pain you're far more likely to avoid situations where you are open and vulnerable. As a result you will also avoid situations where you can learn, develop, grow, and experience real joy. We don't always know how to do this naturally, and there is nothing wrong with getting proper professional help to enable you to do that. Some people will take refuge in their beliefs, whether religious, spiritual or scientific. What seems to be important in terms of happiness is recognising something beyond yourself and the situation that you are in. Charities have been set up as a result of the indescribable pain of the loss of a child, where the founder has discovered strength and a sense of purpose from helping other people in similar situations. It doesn't remove the pain they feel; it does shift the focus onto something positive.

Different is good, we need different!

If you spent all of your time with people who look the same, dress the same, talked the same and felt the same about everything as you do, life would be incredibly boring! The world is full of problems and challenges that we face as human beings living on this planet at this point in time. Each and every one of us is a unique combination of our genetic makeup, our upbringing, and the specific things that we have experienced up until this present moment. This means that there is not, has never been, and can never be another person completely identical to you. If you spend any time reading biographies you will notice is that the things that bring people to the notice of society and biographers are the things that make them different and have brought about the unique contributions that they have made. There is a thread that runs through their life from one experience to another that leads them inexorably towards the difference that they will make in the world.

Let me tell you a story about bees to make this point. Bees pollinate three-quarters of the world's most important crops; we rely on them and other insects to pollinate most of our fruit and vegetables. It would cost UK farmers £1.8 billion to fertilise their plants without them, but bees are under threat due to a number of factors. One cause is the growth of modern agricultural methods using single varieties of crops and large amounts of fertiliser and pesticides. We need a variety of plants for biodiversity. There are areas in the world where there can be no bees because there isn't a wide enough range of plants to support the population. In the United States for example, fully populated beehives are carried on Lorries into the almond tree groves to fertilise the trees, and then driven on to the next orchard. If we lose the bees we lose our crops, if we lose our crops we lose our food, if we lose our food we starve. Variety is vitally important.

We are facing a host of different challenges societally, environmentally, and globally. We need people who see things differently to have the courage and feel secure enough to take a lead so that our world can be a better place. Marianne Williamson[111] wrote the following poem which is often attributed wrongly to Nelson Mandela's inaugural speech:

> *"Our deepest fear is not that we are inadequate.*
> *Our deepest fear is that we are powerful beyond measure.*
> *It is our light, not our darkness that most frightens us.*
> *We ask ourselves, who am I to be brilliant, gorgeous, talented, fabulous?*

---

111 Marianne Williamson, *A Return To Love: Reflections on the Principles of A Course in Miracles*, Harper Collins, 1992. From Chapter 7, Section 3 (Pg. 190-191).

Actually, who are you not to be? You are a child of God.
Your playing small does not serve the world.
There is nothing enlightened about shrinking so that other people won't feel insecure around you.
We are all meant to shine, as children do.
We were born to make manifest the glory of God that is within us.
It's not just in some of us; it's in everyone.
And as we let our own light shine, we unconsciously give other people permission to do the same.
As we are liberated from our own fear, our presence automatically liberates others."

Uncovering the unique person that the world needs to have

As a parent, this is your mission. To discover what is good, valuable, and special about yourself and in doing so learn to recognise the uniqueness and the value in your children. Sometimes it is so much easier to see the good in other people than it is to see it in ourselves, and that's okay. You watch your children for years, looking at their particular pattern of strengths and weaknesses, and you have spent quite a bit of time already helping them to develop and grow. How much more effective can you be once you really understand who they are, what they need, and what their dreams are for the future?

Childhood and adolescence is the perfect time to experiment, try out new things and try new personalities. So this stage isn't about uncovering what they going to do when they're 38, it's about building up a set of skills and abilities, loves and passions that will carry them forward into adult life with joy. Our job is to walk alongside them long enough to find out where those passions lie and to present them with as many opportunities as we can, following the passions that have special meaning and are joyful for them.

Don't worry if the topics that your child is interested in feel a bit niche. It might not mean that there are thousands of jobs out there for them, but it might mean that they can create a career and life that recognises them as a person, and uses their skills in an area that they love.

Voyage of discovery – celebrate what you have learned

No one ever said parenting was easy. There's a good reason for that, it isn't! But if you think about the choices you make, the way you behave and the child that you have, you will learn and develop alongside your child. I firmly believe that in many ways children raise their parents, rather than the other way round. Through my children I have learned to be more open and affectionate. I learned to be more patient than I ever thought possible, and experienced highs and lows that I wouldn't have believed.

Before I had children, I thought that being a parent was about telling them everything I knew. Little did I know that my specialist interests were going to broaden and include (and move through) areas such as the Barbie movies, Lego Bionicles, online gaming and YouTubers. Neither did I think I would understand in detail the joys of antique sword collecting or canoeing and kayaking which I've inherited from my husband!

We have learned ways of being with each other and on our own that are really helpful. We found ways of working as a family together that probably won't suit everyone, and may not work for another family but are tailored to us and are our specific ways of doing things. We are a whole family making 'reasonable adjustments' for each other!

Steering your child through their education

What any child needs will change as they grow and develop, and become easier to supply as a child grows into an adult and what is important for their wellbeing becomes clearer. I was puzzled after I had just given birth to my second child, to learn that he was a very cuddly baby from the midwives. I had had him less than 24 hours and they already knew more about him than I did! I didn't know at that stage that he was cuddlier than some babies, and that some don't like being touched at all. Sometimes the professionals around you have a different perspective, and have seen more children than you, so can spot when something is unusual, or different. The professionals who spend time with your child can help identify what that child is really like from a different point of view. This gives you really good information to add to your own in-depth understanding and helps you to flush out what might be the best solution for them.

Choosing a school is always difficult as we discuss in Chapter 8. Working with friends, family, and other professionals so that you understand not only what your child is like, but also what the options are in your area, gives you a much better chance of finding a good fit between your child and their setting. Do remember, that it is your child you're educating not a smaller version of you. Start from their skills and abilities and personality rather than yours. Having said that though, if you're not comfortable with any setting, for any reason, trust your gut feeling and don't send your child there.

Your child will change, so remember to check what they can do, how they feel and what they like and dislike frequently. What you want in a nursery will be different to what you need when your child reaches primary or secondary school. As they get older, keep picturing them as an adult, remember how far they have come, but be aware that they can still surprise you!

As they grow to be an adult, their level of engagement and responsibility for choosing how they want to spend the rest of their life increases, and yours decreases. Are you willing and able to step back to enable your young person to develop themselves in the direction they want to go? Can you be there as an expert adviser, rather than a director of what they are doing? This is really hard, bearing in mind you have a huge amount of knowledge, skills and life experience that your young person simply doesn't have yet. The best thing you can do, is to share your understanding of how things work, without removing from them the choice to create a life that they want to live.

Creating a family where everyone is loved and valued

Life can be hard out there, and there will be times when nothing is going right. Sometimes, whilst you're trying to make the outside world fit what you need for your child, you need to have something and somewhere safe and peaceful to come back to. Make your home a refuge, where you and your family can find acceptance and challenge within a safe environment. Sometimes, only the people you know really well can tell you things you don't want to hear. I was very struck by hearing Ros Blackburn, an adult with autism, describe how her parents wouldn't let her get away with anything, and how they would challenge her to do better on a daily basis. Although she would much rather spend her time with her special interests (trampolining and ice skating), their firm support has helped her achieve far more. In the final analysis, you do your child no favours if you don't give them the skills to live as best they can in the world.

Working outside of your own comfort zone all of the time is absolutely exhausting. None of us like doing things we are really bad at, or find difficult all of the time. We all need downtime in order for us to regroup, recover, and gather our energies for the next activity. I have noticed how hugely beneficial it is for me to build in parts of the day just for relaxation and play. What that might be will vary from person to person, but for your child it might be a yoga session, ten minutes with a punch bag, or one episode of the programme that they love on television. Don't forget to include downtime for you too! My favourite calming activities are singing, a high intensity workout, cooking, reading a book, and meditation. You will have your own, although it might be a long time since you felt you had time to do them!

Most spiritual teaching agrees that gratitude is important, and there is growing evidence on how good being thankful is for our emotional well-being. I know that when I concentrate on the lovely experiences that I have and the simple pleasures in life I am much happier. When I'm happy, I can be more supportive, focused, and helpful to my family. You don't have to be grateful for the big things (although that helps), it could be something as simple as enjoying a hot cup of coffee, a chat with a friend or the feel of fresh clean clothes on your skin. I don't manage to be grateful all the time, but I have noticed an upsurge in the amount of joy that I feel when I'm thankful for the lovely things I experience. I didn't expect the sense of peace that I get when expressing gratitude even for situations and experiences that brought me pain and sadness.

Living without regret

When we arrive at adulthood, we are the sum total of the skills, abilities and experiences we have had up to that point. When I was 16, I thought being right was more important than being kind or being happy. My father's mother was a skittish, birdlike woman who loved nature. She had hurt her leg climbing over a fence when she was trying to do something on her own. I enjoyed telling her off for not having asked for help, was revelling in being able to tell off a grown-up and was surprised to find that I had upset her. She accused me of being very hard as she cried softly and she was right. I didn't know then how important independence was to her, what she needed, and how her horizons were shrinking as she grew older. Although she died over 14 years ago now, I wish I had been kinder. I learnt through that and many other experiences that it is far more important to be kind than it is to be right. I like the person I am now much better as a result.

In the business of everyday life, it's easy to forget the impact we have on other people and how important the way that you behave is in terms of their wellbeing. I remember the awful example of a mother whose last words to her son were angry because he hadn't done something around the house. He left for school and was killed by a car walking home. She has to live with that for the rest of her life. When my children drive me to distraction, I hear that in my head, and remember that whatever stupid, careless or ungrateful thing they have done is less important than the fact that they know they are loved, even on the days that I'm not at all sure that I like what they are or aren't doing!

This approach doesn't mean ignoring the things that they do that are wrong, but it does mean dealing with them in a way that separates their behaviour from who they are and the fact that you still love them. You will still need to have conversations about what you expect from them and how you expect to be treated, but if you frame those in a way that values both their feelings and yours, you are modelling an approach that is emotionally aware and opens up the possibility for an honest dialogue. I have been amazed by how well my children have responded to this approach, but fully realise that it might not work as well for everybody.

Dying at peace, knowing that your child will be OK

No-one enjoys thinking about their own death and a time that they will not be around, but if you have a child with special needs, especially if they are profoundly affected, you might not have the same expectations that most parents have for them growing up, finding a partner and living independently. The first thing to say is that you may well be surprised at how well they could cope if given the right support. I would not wish to suggest that process is straightforward or simple, but it is increasingly possible. Many children with special needs will live an independent life that is every bit as successful as those without any issues. As with all things in this field, it is always better to start preparing for that day early, by giving your young person as many personal skills as you can and putting in place multi-layered support for them. We do know that the most protective placement for young people with profound and multiple disabilities is one where they have a strong community around them beyond their residential placement.

There are a number of things that you will need to prepare:

- Where would they like to be and what would they like to do?
- Where they will live – can they live in your home or do you need to find an independent placement?
- Financial planning – what resources do you have access to that can help?
- Do they have a friendship group?
- Are there any other family members around who would take responsibility for overseeing their care?
- Do they have independence skills?
- Could they live independently, on their own or with support?
- Do they have activities that they love to do in the community?
- Can they carry out meaningful paid employment (with support or independently)?
- Can they make choices and express preferences effectively?
- How street-smart are they?

Some of these issues are really hard to get to grips with for anybody, but especially so for those with special needs and doubly so for those with complex and profound difficulties. What we do know, is that the earlier you start building the skills that you want to see in whatever ways are possible and appropriate to the development of your child, the more likely they are to be able to demonstrate those skills in later life. So start early, break it down, and build them up for the future. When you can see in hundreds of little ways, your young person blossoming into the sort of person you really hoped they could be, even if that picture is different to how you once thought it might have looked, then it becomes possible to start the process of accepting the probability that they will need to live without you. Given the loving care you have given them for so many years, you need to believe that they will be okay. Do everything you possibly can and then have faith in the fact that it will be enough and finally learn to be at peace.

Learning to let go

As a parent, one of the hardest things to accept is that our children have to grow away from us in order to be the people they need to be. We nurtured them when they were tiny, looked out for them, watched them as they grew, protected them from danger as best we can. This instinct is incredibly strong in parents. We are hardwired to protect the next generation. So it's not surprising that learning to give them space to grow and develop is hard. From the moment they start to walk and can go in whatever direction they want, rather than the direction we take them, we are hyper vigilant to the dangers they might face.

In many ways, raising a child is a long, slow process of learning to let go. As they get older and are more able then we have to allow them more freedom to act and choose where they want to go, and what they want to do. This process is hard for all parents, but it is especially hard if your child has special needs and is struggling. It can feel almost impossible if your child has very high support needs and you are caring for them in a more intense way on a daily basis. But if we don't allow them any space, they can't grow and develop. Sometimes, the professionals who work with our children can help us to see the potential for them to be more than they are at the moment – that they may be capable of doing more than we ask of them. It's worth listening to other people as well as hearing your own fear about what could go wrong.

Learning how to try new things, behave in new ways, and have new experiences is a key part of what it is to be human. For some of our young people, especially those in special residential care, their worlds can be very restricted and very small. If we want to prepare for young people for as independent a life as possible, we need to have the highest possible expectations for them and to lift their horizons so that they can see more, try more and love more. Parents can give their children the gift of freedom of choice. As they grow and develop (at whatever age), our children become adults who can open up new horizons for themselves.

Glossary of Terms and Titles

ADD – Attention Deficit Disorder. A subtype of ADHD but without the restless fidgeting, people with ADD tend to be dreamy and inattentive, easily distracted with poor organisational skills.

ADHD – Attention Deficit Hyperactivity Disorder. People with ADHD have a short attention span, are easily distracted, restless with constant fidgeting and tend to be impulsive.

Asperger Syndrome – Asperger syndrome is a form of autism which is a lifelong disability that affects how a person makes sense of the world, processes information and relates to other people. Autism is often described as a 'spectrum disorder' because the condition affects people in many different ways and to varying degrees.

Autism – Autism is a lifelong developmental disability that affects how a person communicates with, and relates to, other people. It also affects how they make sense of the world around them. It is a spectrum condition, which means that, while all autistic people share certain difficulties, their condition will affect them in different ways. Some autistic people are able to live relatively independent lives but others may have accompanying learning disabilities and need a lifetime of specialist support. People with autism may also experience over- or under-sensitivity to light, touch, sounds, tastes, smells, or colours.

Autistic Disorder – A diagnostic label used when someone fits the full picture of typical autism.

Atypical Autism – The diagnostic label used when someone meets some, but not all of the criteria for typical autism.

Child and Adolescent Mental Health Services (CAMHS) – A specialist UK National Health Service provision. They offer assessment and treatment when children and young people have emotional, behavioural or mental health difficulties including ADHD and autism.

Childhood Autism – A diagnostic label used when a child fits the full picture of typical autism.

Clinical Psychologist – Clinical psychologists aim to reduce psychological distress in people with mental or physical health problems or learning disabilities.

Developmental Coordination Disorder (DCD) – A common disorder that affects movement and co-ordination and includes Dyspraxia.

Disability – A disability is a physical or mental impairment that has a 'substantial' and 'long-term' negative effect on your ability to do normal daily activities.

Dyslexia – Dyslexia is a learning difficulty that primarily affects the skills involved in accurate and fluent word reading and spelling.

Dyspraxia – Dyspraxia, a form of developmental coordination disorder (DCD) is a common disorder affecting fine and/or gross motor coordination in children and adults. It may also affect speech. DCD is a lifelong condition.

Education Health & Care Plan (EHC Plan) – A document that replaces a Statement of SEN, but can start at birth and continue until the young person is 25. It covers Education, Social Care and Health provision within a single document.

Educational Psychologist (Ed Psych) – A specialist Psychologist who works with children and young people usually between 0-19 years of age experiencing difficulties. For example, they may work to promote learning, develop emotional, social and behavioural skills and support psychological development.

High Functioning Autism (HFA) – A diagnostic term used for someone with autism, with average or above average intelligence who may have had significant language delay which is the main differentiator between High Functioning Autism and Asperger syndrome.

Individual Education Plan (IEP) – An IEP is a document that helps teaching staff to plan for your child, teach him, and review his progress. IEPs are different for each child and should set out what should be taught, how it should be taught and how often.

Intellectual Disability – Term used in the USA and Canada for Learning Disabilities.

Learning Difficulty – Often used to describe conditions including dyslexia, dyspraxia, ADHD, ADD, dyscalculia, which affects the way information is learned and processed. They are neurological (rather than psychological), usually run in families and occur independently of intelligence. They can have significant impact on education, learning and literacy skills.

Learning Disabilities – Where a person has a significantly reduced ability to understand new or complex information, to learn new skills and a reduced ability to cope independently which starts before adulthood with lasting effects on development.

Neurodiverse – Neurodiverse is a non-judgemental term used to describe anyone with autism, ADHD, dyslexia or anyone with a condition that is based on a variety in how their brain works.

Neurodiversity – A term favoured by autistic adults which sees autism as a particular way of being and their neurodiversity as positive rather than negative.

Neurotypical – A term given to individuals without autism or other neurodevelopmental conditions.

Paediatrician – A medical doctor specialising in the treatment of children.

Pathological Demand Avoidance (PDA) – Someone who is diagnosed with PDA is considered as being on the autism spectrum (even though they can appear to have much better social understanding and communication skills), but the main difficulty is that they are driven to avoid the demands and expectations of everyday life in order to reduce their levels of anxiety.

Pervasive Developmental Disorder – Not Otherwise Specified (PDD-NOS) – Diagnostic term used to describe someone whose behaviour fits most, but not all, of the criteria for typical autism.

Provision Map – Similar to an IEP (See above), a provision map identifies what support a specific child with SEN needs. Provision maps can also be used by schools to plan for small groups, classes or the whole school.

Semantic-Pragmatic Disorder – A term used to describe someone who finds it hard to understand the meaning of phrases and sentences, taking them literally and how to use language socially (e.g turn-taking, interruping, talking off-topic and giving too much or too little information.)

Special Educational Needs (SEN) – The term used to describe a pupil who requires additional or different educational support from other children of the same age.

Special Educational Needs Coordinator (SENCO) – Within a school, the SENCO will be the person responsible for the day-to-day operation of the school's Special Educational Needs Policy. All mainstream schools must appoint a teacher to be their SENCO.

SEND – **Special Educational Needs and Disabilities**. A broader definition of SEN (see above) that includes disabilities.

Sensory Sensitivities – A difference in the way that an individual experiences information received by their senses. They can be over or under sensitive to things that they see, smell, hear, taste, touch and may have problems with their balance and the position of their body in space.

Speech and Language Therapist – Speech and language therapists (also known as SLT or SALT) assess and treat speech, language and communication problems in people of all ages to help them better communicate. They'll also work with people who have eating and swallowing problems.

SLCN – **Speech and Language Communication Needs (SLCN)** A child with speech, language and communication needs might have speech that is difficult to understand, might struggle to say words or sentences, may not understand words that are being used, or the instructions they hear or may have difficulties knowing how to talk and listen to others in a conversation.

Statement – A statement of Special Educational Needs was the system whereby a child would be given specific support and was funded by a Local Authority. It sometimes detailed a 'named school' and was the highest level of support for SEN. It has been replaced from September 2014 by the Education Health and Care Plan (EHCP).

Occupational Therapist – Occupational therapists work with people of all ages to help them overcome the effects of disability caused by physical or psychological illness, ageing or accident.

Wave 1, 2 and 3 Provision – Used in provision mapping in schools (see above), it details the interventions that a school is planning to put into place. Wave 1 is whole school, wave 2 for small groups of children and wave 3 for an individual child.

Last words and thanks

Thank you for reading my book. I hope that it has reminded you how resourceful you can be and given you some useful ideas of where to look for more information, help and support. If you enjoyed it, please tell your friends, family, professionals, the postman and everyone else and don't forget to take a moment to leave me a review at your favourite online bookshop!

Connect with Sarah-Jane Critchley

Email me: Sarah-Jane@differentjoy.com

Look at my website: www.different.joy.com

Follow me on Twitter: www.twitter.com/@SarahJaneCritch

Favorite me at Smashwords: www.smashwords.com/profile/view/writingscorp67

Different Joy Club

Sign up at www.differentjoy.com/different-joy-club-2/ to get the latest and best information I have available.

Notes

Notes

29133372R00118

Printed in Great Britain
by Amazon